Russia's Road to Modernity

Russia's Road to Modernity

by

Jerzy Gierus

Strategic Book Publishing and Rights Co.

Strategic Book Publishing and Rights Co.
12620 FM 1960, Suite A4-507
Houston, TX 77065
www.sbpra.com

ISBN: 978-1-62516-313-4

Bad men have no songs.
How is it the Russians have songs?

Friedrich Nietzsche
Maxims and Arrows, Twilight of the Idols.

Contents

Preface

The present work is an attempt to look at Russian social change through the prism of modernisation theory. Now that the communist experiment has been totally discredited and the countries that were involved in it are wholeheartedly reaching for the values of western-type liberalism and market economy, a broad conceptual framework is needed to interpret the forces that drove them into communism and those that are at work during post-communist transformation. It is the thesis of this work that the forces operating in the first and second cases are the same. They are the dynamics of modernity, and the world system as one of the main institutional expressions of it. To understand the processes of the present day social transformation, it is crucial to know *what* society is being transformed and in what circumstances this transformation is taking place.

Our understanding of modernisation in this work is very broad. We see modernisation as a spread of rational attitudes and practices since Judaism and early Christianity. This is most fully expressed in the formation of the ethics of Protestantism and reaches structural fruition in the form of modern institutions. The term "transformation" as I use it in this work is broad and means social change as such. This work examines how the mechanisms of modernity influenced social change in Russia over a wide time span. The most crucial point of change, when the driving forces of modernity were particularly vivid, was the turn of the twentieth century. Therefore we devote special attention to this period. Much of what happened in Russia thereafter—the communist rule and breaking out from it—can be clearly seen in the light of the trends and events of the turn of the century.

Since the early sixteenth century, modernity began to spread vigorously from the countries of north-Western Europe, and the world became clearly divided into two distinct parts—the core and the periphery. The periphery became dependent on the core and had to adjust to the trends coming from it. Being linked to the core by the ties established in the course of global centralisation, the periphery had to transplant onto its soil numerous institutions, and hence values, outlooks, and attitudes, which originated and were native to the core. Wherever these modern institutions confronted a traditional peasant-based environment, i.e., wherever there was no social base for their transplantation, their meaning was modified by the *milieu* in which they were placed. Institutional surrogates emerged that consisted of the closely entangled modern and traditional elements. Nominally they were often equivalents of respective core-like institutions, i.e., parliament, political party, democracy, etc. Their functioning, however, was of an essentially different kind.

There also appeared nominally new concepts and institutions, like socialist democracy, communist morality, planned economy, party of a new type, etc. As we try to argue in this work, they were also institutional surrogates, bringing together the elements of modernity and tradition. The existence of such social, economic, and cultural aggregates, and the fact that they didn't serve the purposes to which they were called, gave the observer the impression of their unreality and ghostliness. Max Weber, observing the Russian political scene at the turn of the twentieth century, called it *Scheinkonstitutionalismus* and *Scheindemokratie*. In this work, we attach more examples of such institutional substitutes.

The first part deals with the problem of Russia's identity. It compares Russian preoccupation with her role in the world in the late nineteenth century and at present and asks the question about the nature of such preoccupation and whether it was characteristic of Russia alone. The technique proposed to gain insight into

Russian social paradigm is Weber's analytical method. It suggests splitting it into discrete parts, describing each part with the help of the specially constructed ideal types, and then trying to define the whole in the light of the insights gained. The ideal types constructed are those of traditional and modern society. The description of the way in which modernity is diffused closes Part One.

The second part is an illustration of different mergers of traditional and modern elements in Russian social, political, cultural, and economic spheres. The obtained constructs, or aggregates, or Braudelian *ensembles* are institutional and cultural substitutes, or surrogates of modern structures and attitudes that originated in the West. The special attention given to Russian nineteenth century literature is explained by the fact that culture was the main medium through which the meaning of modern institutions and postures was filtered. It is argued that often in Russian history, literary stances substituted for civic and political ones, and literary public sphere stood for political public sphere.

In the third part, we try to name the social reality composed of the identified surrogates and answer the questions posed in Part One. Our conclusions are: first, the Russian social model since the mid-nineteenth century and throughout the communist period suits Jowitt's description of the "dependent society"; second, there is much evidence in support of Teodor Shanin's thesis that Russia at the turn of the twentieth century became the first country ever to evince the syndrome of what later became known as "developing society;" third, Russia's "uniqueness," proclaimed by her nationalist-minded intellectuals was a "regional myth," the creation of which was a common affair among the countries of the world's periphery at the time of the formation and consolidation of nation-states. Further in Part Three, we bring some historical facts that explain how Russia found herself in a peripheral position. In the conclusion of Part Three, we outline the settings, in which Russian present transformation is taking place, and formulate a thesis that important further developments will be influenced by a general tendency towards universalisation and the creation of global institutional spheres.

In the writing of this book, I have tried to refer to what has commonly been called "Russian damned questions"—the questions that have obsessed Russian intellectuals and thinkers from times immemorial and that cut through Russian moral and political philosophy, torment Russian literary heroes, and are the subject of everyday social conversations at kitchen tables as well as on television programs. These are the questions that reflect what Russia is all about: How is it different from the rest of the world, is it better or worse than the West, what is this thing called "Russian soul," does the West have a "soul," do Russian people have a special sort of humanity that is superior to everybody else, in what way was the appearance and existence of this humanity influenced by the Russian Orthodox church, etc. The answers given to these questions range from the point of extreme nationalism and great Russian imperial pride as instanced by nationalist ideology present in the writings of such authors as Dostoyevsky or Berdiaev, to extreme pessimism and humiliation best illustrated by Chaadaev's, *Philosophical Letters*. The debate has persisted into the twenty-first century and has acquired additional eloquence and brilliance in the arguments put forward by Russian present day pro- and anti-West thinkers appearing in the newly-free media. The debate has become, not only more free and open, but has gained a new edge from the recent experience of living in a totally closed and inward-looking society in which the option of a self-contained social structure based on a classical Platonic model of state was attempted to be merged with a model of a modern American-type democracy.

What the communist experience seems to have taught Russian present-day thinkers is that the world outside Russia never ceased to develop and that Russia has always been involved in the process of taking a stance towards what appeared on the international scene, be it in the sphere of culture, politics, or technology. Various responses to the challenges these developments elicited are now assessed in new ways and conclusions drawn seem to be based on more realistic and pragmatic grounds. Greater awareness seems to be present in Russia of living in an increasingly unified world where nothing is wholly unique, but is related to, composed of, or built on the model of something else. This marks a new stage in forming a civil society that does not pretend to be something exceptional and superior, but accepts that it is like the rest of societies of human beings and reaches for the dialogue with them on the basis of common understanding on personal and institutional levels.

In a sense, Russia is now in the process of acquiring a new perception of the meaning of politics. The nineteenth century nationalist awakening led Russian intellectuals to look for the model of their country's development in classical antiquity. They did this in parallel with other continental European thinkers for whom a blueprint for society was the classical model. It was built from the top down, strictly hierarchical, and controlled by outstanding men. The rest of the populace were expected to follow these leaders in implementing such a model.

It was a mark of the nineteenth century that such great men were thought, not only to possess superior minds and outstanding political instincts, but also to be the best and most genuine representatives of the totality of the tight community— the nation. This belonging to the nation was the ultimate source of energy and inspiration necessary to organise human beings for living together. It was believed the ancient Greeks and Romans had felt the same about their own societies and consequently harboured superiority to other "nations."

What had escaped continental European political thinkers was that the classical national and imperial pride came on top of purely technical and scrupulously defined principles of how human groups are and ought to be organised. What eluded them was that the human being is fundamentally a *political animal* and the source of his pride is or should be in how just, fair, and acceptable the principles of living together are. Once they prove to be so, there are legitimate reasons to extol their worth and the virtues of those who put them in place and who abide by them. When it happens the other way round, a society is driven into a virtuous circle from which it finds it extremely difficult to liberate itself. The cart is then put before the horse, the answer is put before the question, and the emotion is put before the thought. Gloom then descends on the people, their perception of reality becomes distorted, and the *damned questions* begin to abound.

The return from the deadlock is possible when people rediscover the true and original meaning of politics. This seems to be taking place regularly in the course of human history especially when the plunge is particularly severe. Such rediscovery of what politics really means seems to be at the centre of great social upheavals and revolutions. Few of them have managed to restore the true principles governing human nature and society. One of the success stories was the American Revolution that gave birth to a free, prosperous, and efficient society. Most subsequent revolutions were not so successful. They started off with the example of the American Revolution in mind, but ended with the effects of the French Revolution. The vicious circle was too hard to break. The Russian Revolution was no exception. New social uprisings in the Arab world in the second decade of the twenty-first century will probably go no farther, judging by the way the old mistakes are repeated by the elites of newly-free societies. It is the intention of this book to throw some light on the functioning mechanisms of peripheral societies driven by a genuine longing to find the correct path to proceed and by the ambition of their intellectual elites to build a modern and progressive social structure while having the best existing models in view. The specific society under scrutiny is Russia. The conclusions arrived at and the lessons drawn may concern any society that aspires to modernise.

Jerzy Gierus

***

Part One: The identity

Chapter One

The Nature of Russia's Otherness

The ways of studying Russia

There is no shortage of literature about Russia. This country has received attention from scholars not just because of her geographical vastness and importance in international relations, but also because there was always an air of some mystery and ambiguity about her. As a giant Euro-Asian power placed outside of the core of European countries, she became a focus of characteristics that distinguished her both from the countries of Europe and those of Asia. Russia's centuries long self-isolation and the closed nature of her society intensified her strangeness in the eyes of the world.

The study of Russia developed along with the development of social sciences as such. Different approaches were used in writing about her at different times. There is no doubt that we know much more about her now than we did before and that she has lost much of the mysterious air she used to possess. We cannot be positive, however, that all questions have been answered. As Russia opens up to the world that is undergoing rapid change, many things appear in a new light and many new questions present themselves.

Historically, there were various methodologies to describe Russia. Those who analysed her by looking from the inside—beginning with the writers, historians, and philosophers of the nineteenth century and ending with the contemporary ones—were polarised into two main groups. The first group, the Slavophiles, tended to mystify Russia and present her as a proverbial sphinx—not to be understood rationally, but only to be experienced emotionally and through faith. Most of the writers of this category stood on the ground of Russian Orthodox religion that cemented their ideology and served as an agent of its dissemination among the broad strata of the society. The main crux of this ideology was the conception of Russians as the chosen people who upheld the ideals of humanity in an increasingly materialistic and dehumanised world. Russia was perceived as the third Rome, the messianic nation called to save the world that had gone astray. The outside world was identified mainly with Roman Catholicism which, according to Dostoyevsky, had "yielded to the second temptation of the devil," i.e., had exchanged spiritual values for earthly riches.

This view of Russia, counterbalanced though it was by the diametrically opposite doctrine of the "Westerners," the other main ideology of Russian intellectuals, has left deep roots in Russian thinking and added to the belief that Russia was something special and distinct from the rest of the world in some important way. This belief was so strong and so widespread, that people inside Russia of different, often opposite, political persuasions are up until now not entirely free from it. Good or bad, they argue, Russia is not like anybody else.

Among western conceptualisations, Russia figured in different theoretical systems. Marx approached Russia from the point of view of the concept of "Asiatic economy" or "Asiatic mode of production." This was echoed by Lenin who was well aware of Russia's backwardness and her remoteness from European economic and cultural models. Such a view was present in most western analytical writing that stressed the role in Russia of the despotic state, pointed to her slow economic growth, and the underdevelopment of her social sphere. A Harvard historian, Richard Pipes, called the Russian historical model "patrimonial state,"[1] meaning that the tsars regarded the whole of the country as their property and acted accordingly. This attitude according to Pipes was characteristic also to the Soviet rulers.

Another trend in western thinking about Russia concentrated on the nature of Russian Orthodox religion. A historian, Arnold Toynbee, for example, saw Russia as belonging to "Orthodox civilisation," distinct from western Christendom. Such a view didn't involve much evaluation, and simply placed Russia among other civilisations classified in accordance with the principle of religious culture.

Much literature was devoted to analysis of the Soviet political system. The authors writing on this subject saw communist rule either as a continuation of Russian tradition of grass roots communalism combined with the despotism of her rulers, or as a new development caused by the spread of western radical ideas about state and society. The communist period was often divided into stages. An American historian, Robert Tucker, for example, saw a radically new quality in the post-Stalin period. According to him, Stalinist terror was mainly a projection of Stalin's personal psychopathology. Accordingly, in Tucker's view, Stalin's death opened the prospect for a relatively peaceful process of social engineering aimed at the building of a Russian social order that would best suit this country's cultural traditions. Those traditions, thought Tucker, were not inherently despotic or evil and Russia stood a fair chance of becoming a reasonably civilised and well-to-do European country capable of exercising her influence and power in a responsible way. An important reason for believing so is the existence of a great Russian cultural tradition and her achievements in the arts and sciences. Given this basis, Russia can go a long way in developing a thriving public sphere and balancing off her tendency toward a despotic rule with an enlightened concern for the overall wellbeing. Tucker's diagnosis was made in the wake of the death of Stalin

---

1   See R. Pipes: *Russia under the Old Regime,* Harmondsworth 1982.

and at the time when new trends in Soviet policies began to emerge following Khrushchev's famous unmasking speech and the publication of documents testifying to the criminal nature of Stalin's regime.

The end of communist rule in Russia opened up new prospects for historical interpretations. It turned out that although the Bolshevik-established political system had the appearance of a historical novelty, what stood behind it was not altogether new. The trends that were active in the western world ever since the late nineteenth century (and the ground for which was prepared much earlier) were also working in Russia. Their influence, however, was more covert. They got entangled with indigenous trends and produced attitudes and institutions that only appeared to be of a new and different order.

To evaluate the present-day Russian transformation, references should therefore necessarily be made to her past and to the events elsewhere in the world that exercised an influence on her. In fact, outside influences on Russia have been decisive throughout her whole history. The role of the Normans in the building of the first Russian state, the introduction of Christianity from Byzantium, the crippling yoke of Mongol-Tatars, the pro-western reforms of Peter the Great, the ideological ferment (with crucial practical consequences caused by the indulgence with western nineteenth century schools of thought), and the readiness to accept the ideals of liberal democracy in the post-Gorbachev era of social reforms—all these facts point to the pivotal role of the outside factor in Russian history. Any credible, present-day social analysis of Russia has to take these considerations into account.

Has Russia got an identity problem?

A well-known Russian historical philosopher, Nikolai Danilevsky, in the opening passages of his book, *Russia and Europe,*[2] describes military action undertaken by Russian

---

2   N.Y.Danilevsky: *Rossia i Evropa*, Moskva 1869.

troops in the mid-nineteenth century to intervene into Turkey to protect the interests of the Orthodox population there, who were believed to be suffering under Muslim oppression. What the Russian government and most of the Russian public opinion considered as legitimate and necessary measures were met with severe criticism from the West. Outrage was generated among the European public and politicians, who, in Danilevsky's view, were not half that scrupulous when similar things had happened in their own backyard. He cites numerous occasions when European governments suppressed independence movements in their own allegedly egotistic interests and, not only got away with it, but managed to convince the public that their actions were good, civilised, and legal. Danilevsky concludes that there is a profound difference in attitude between Russia and the West and proceeds to examine the nature of it.

He is the first to have introduced the philosophy of history as a series of distinct civilisations that he called "cultural-historical types." Russia belonged to the type that had only recently made itself visible by coming forward with the culture in which its rightness and humanity superseded the old, outgoing western civilisations. These new values, he maintained, were in the process of being formulated and only the future could show whether they would prove resilient and would replace the values produced by old Europe.

Clearly, Danilevsky's theory falls neither into the distinct category of the teachings of the Slavophiles, nor into those of the Westerners. He is less convinced about the destiny of the Russians to become the teachers of humanity as are the former, and, while giving credit to historical achievements of western civilisation, he rejects its basic principles as formalistic, inhuman, and hypocritical. What is important about his outlook is that it reflects the state of the Russian intellectual mind at this very critical moment in history and puts the question in the most straightforward way: How does Russia compare with the West? Will she be able to preserve her values at a time when they are under the threat from rational and self-interested attitudes of the West?

The questions asked directly and indirectly by Danilevsky marked for Russia the coming to the end of one epoch and the beginning of another. It was not so long before these academic deliberations acquired a sinister form of major political upheavals and brought Russia the reality, which many nineteenth century academics couldn't have imagined even in their worst nightmares. These questions, however, would be doomed to remain the "damned questions" that the Russian intellectuals persistently asked over and over again, suggesting more than just academic interest.

The events, similar to those that Danilevsky described in the introduction to his great work, will also occur in the new settings of the technological twentieth century such as Afghanistan, Chechnya, Baku, and Vilnius. New generations of Russian intellectuals will ask what is so wrong in defending Russian legitimate interests in some far-off Caucasian republic, or why is it the business of the West to criticise Russian action in defence of her vital interests. The overtones of these new discussions will be different as much as the surrounding world will be a different place. However, the search of Russian intellectuals for their country's place in the world will still continue.

The present work will try to discover what underlies such obsession with identity. We shall compare these reactions with the reactions of intellectuals in other parts of the world. We shall place Russia in a broad international context and examine her development in the light of religious identity, political economy, social structure, etc.

The question that we shall try to answer is whether Russia can be viewed as a "special case" in mankind's history as Slavophiles insist it can. It seems obvious that natural conditions, such as geography and climate, as well as ethnogenesis add up to specificity of any nation. We shall address these issues first. Then we shall proceed with the issues of historical, social, and cultural character, for it is in this sphere that the Slavophiles (and not only them) tend to see the main focus of features that make Russia different from the rest of the world.

Geographical position

Geographically, Russia is partly in Europe and partly in Asia. There are two main geographic features that make Europe different from other regions of the world, especially from Asia; these are: first, diversity of the terrain and, second, marked sinuosity of her sea edge contours. Nowhere do mountains, plains, and valleys intermix so often and on so small an area. On the other hand, deep bays, protruding peninsulas, and capes form the coastal relief of Western and Southern Europe. There, for thirty square miles inland, there is one mile of seacoast, whereas in Asia for one mile of seacoast, there are one hundred square miles inland.

Russia—we are talking about European Russia—does not share with the rest of Europe the above favourable natural characteristics. The seacoast line makes up only a small measure of her natural boundaries and monotony is the distinguishing feature of her inland surface; one form dominates almost exclusively throughout its extension - the plain, stretching for about ninety thousand square miles and equal to more than nine times the area of France.

The hydrography of Russia, i.e., the network of her rivers, influenced in a decisive manner the mode of settlement of population. The mutual proximity of the main river basins prevented the population settlements from isolation in "hydrographic cages" (to use the phrase coined by the Russian historian, V. Klyuchevsky), but stimulated communication and facilitated collective behavioural patterns.

The millennium-old and hostile coexistence with aggressive Asian tribes was another geographical factor of importance during the formative period of Russian social and cultural identity. The historic product of the steppe, to quote Klyuchevsky, "was the Kosak [...], the homeless, free-wheeling (*gulashchij*) personage, despising social ties outside his group of comrades, the hothead ready to fight the unfaithful, able to destroy but unwilling to build—the historic heir of ancient Kievan knights (*bogatyri*)."[3]

The monotony of the Russian plain contrasts sharply with the diversity of the Western European landscape. The impressions of Russian nineteenth century travellers to the West were those of "enclosed space, rigid definitiveness, and ubiquitous presence of man with impressive evidence of his hard and persistent labour."[4] The traveller then easily recalled his own native Tula or Orel landscape, "marked by gentleness, imperceptibility of contours, even shyness of colours and tones, which produce an indistinct, peacefully-inarticulate impression."[5] The climate of central Russia had been characterised by long and cold winters and rather dry summers, followed by protracted periods of rainfall, which obstructed fieldwork and necessitated speedy harvests. These features, as reflected by Richard Pipes, can account for a certain eruptiveness of the Russian character.

Russian *ethnogenesis* incorporates Slav, Finn, and Turkish elements. They were welded together in a massive process of consolidation and "extended reproduction" of cultural patterns, language usage, fundamental symbols of identification, and self-identification. The major role in construction and delimitation of the Russian ethnos was played by the Orthodox Church. Having acquired a momentum of its own, this homogeneity became of major importance for the history of Russia. It was of central importance for the Russian state's strategy not only to rule by force and suppression, but also through mute consensus of the majority of the population, whose loyalties it used in times of crisis.

---

3   V.O. Kliucevsky: *Kurs russkoi istorii*, part I, Moskva 1987, p. 85.
4   Ibidem, p. 87.
5   Ibidem, p. 92.

Chapter Two

Methodological Approach

Weber's analytical technique

Turning away from natural peculiarities, we step on the ground of social and cultural issues, the sphere most marked by contention and controversy. To answer the question about Russia's uniqueness, we must first turn to the issues of methodological character.

In proceeding with our analysis, we shall make use of the Weberian method that lays emphasis on the understanding of subjective intentions of the actor while also leaving room for structural explanations. Weber's methodology, inspired by the ideals of the Enlightenment, makes the individual person the point of departure and the ultimate unit of analysis:

"Interpretative sociology considers the individual [Einzelnindividuum] and his action as the basic unit, as its 'atom'—if the disputable comparison for once may be permitted. In this approach, the individual is also the upper limit and the sole carrier of meaningful conduct . . .In general, for sociology, such concepts as 'state,' 'association,' 'feudalism,' and the like, designate certain categories of human interaction. Hence it is the task of sociology to reduce these concepts to 'understandable' action, that is, without exception, to the actions of participating individual men."[6]

---

6   M. Weber. *Economy and Society.* New York 1968.

What this emphasis on the individual invokes is the approach of classical economists, with Robinson Crusoe as a human example to illustrate it. It should be distinguished from the Hegelian tradition of "interpretation," seeing the individual person, institution, or act as a manifestation of a larger morphological unit. "Interpretation" in this context means the establishment of the union between the whole and the part that is merely an expression and documentation of the whole.

"Understanding" for Weber meant becoming aware of one's own intentions through introspection and interpreting other people's behaviour in terms of their declared or ascribed intentions. Thus he distinguishes between three main types of motivated actions. The first type, most easily "understandable" according to Weber, is the type of actions, which are caused by rational motives. The person imbued with, and acting according to these motivations, is what we use to call "economic man."

The actions of a less rational kind are motivated by affectual sentiments or by tradition and are directed at the pursuit of "absolute ends." These absolute ends, however, may be pursued by fairly rational means. "Affectual" action flows purely from sentiment and is a less rational type of conduct than "traditional" action, which is unreflective, habitual, and sanctified by ritual.

Weber's "understanding sociology," it may seem, hardly allows any room for structural explanations. These, however, are also present. He refuted the German stereotypical vision of America as a nation of "atomised individuals," but perceived American *democracy* as a complex of exclusive, but voluntary, *associations*. Similarly, he linked the spread of bureaucracies to the task of administering large inland empires, such as Rome, China, Russia, and the United States.

Weber's rejection of the existence of any "objective meaning" also does not preclude his being aware of the paradoxical fact that the results of interactions are not always identical with what the actor intended to do. A graphic example of this is the Puritans; they wished to serve God, but ultimately helped bring about modern capitalism. Another example is the following passage concerning capitalism and the individual:

"This masterless slavery in which capitalism enmeshes the worker or the debtor is only debatable ethically as an institution. In principle, the personal conduct of those who participate, on either side of the rulers or of the ruled, is not morally debatable; as such conduct is essentially prescribed by objective situations. If they do not conform, they are threatened by economic bankruptcy that would, in every respect, be useless."[7]

As we see, Weber is neither an idealist interpreter of history, nor an historical materialist. He seems to avoid any philosophical emphasis on either material or ideal factors, or upon either structural or individual explanations. Speaking about an historical phenomenon, he sees it as a specific combination of certain general factors. These factors are quantifiable and can be present in other unique combinations. "Of course, in the last analysis, all qualitative contrasts in reality can somehow be comprehended as purely quantitative differences made up of combinations of various single factors."[8] This does not mean that quality can be reduced to quantity. What it means is that a cultural reality *is* qualitatively unique; however qualitative differences are produced by quantitative changes.

In order to analyse some entity, we can decompose it into separate elements, which we can then subject to description. To do this, Weber employed logically precise conceptions or "ideal types." These are the logically controlled and pure conceptions describing extreme cases. They are used as methodological instruments to single out parts of empirical reality that exists independently and can only be outlined in general terms.

---

7   Ibidem, p. 235.
8   Ibidem, p. 308.

Closely tied with the quantitative approach to unique cultural entities and the conception of ideal types in Weber's methodology is the comparative method. It implies that a number of constellations can be compared in terms of some feature common to them. This common feature is singled out analytically and runs as a core in his comparative analysis. For example, having approached the analysis of modern society, Weber defines "democracy" as "minimisation of power." He then classifies different historical cases according to the mode of application of this principle, such as short term of office, referendum, functions of parliament, etc. By incorporating historical features into the general conception of democracy, he reduces the general type to something that approximates historical cases.

Now, we shall try to employ the described Weberian technique in our analysis, which is aimed at answering the question posed by Russian nineteenth-century thinkers. We shall ask the question as it was then formulated: In what way, if at all, can Russia be called a unique society, different in substance from any other society? Stemming from this main question will be subordinate questions: Why was this question asked in Russia and persisted for such a long time? Was it asked in a similar way in any other part of the world? Are there any social conditions for this question being asked anywhere? If it was asked somewhere else, did the discussion of it proceed in the same manner as in Russia?

In trying to answer the main question first of all, we shall place Russia in a broad international context and examine her reaction to the trend that began to emanate from Western Europe and spread all around the globe—the development of modernity. Having chosen modernity as a general concept for our comparative analysis, we shall also make use of ideal types of modern and traditional society and see to what extent their features were present in the Russia of the nineteenth century and afterwards. Put differently, the concepts of modern and traditional society will enable us to split the Russian socio-cultural constellation into discrete elements, assess their quantitative presence, and then, if possible, define it.

The theory of modernity

In his brilliant study of early capitalism, Fernand Braudel points out that in the sixteenth century, the populated areas of the world were very close to each other in terms of economic development. The gap between Western Europe and the rest of the world appeared "late in time" and to explain it would be to solve one the greatest mysteries of the world.[9]

One of the approaches to solve this mystery was offered by what, very broadly, is called modernisation theory. In a narrower sense, it came to be identified with theoretical efforts since World War II to explain the rapid growth of the developing societies of Asia, Africa, and Latin America. In this context, it appeared as an alternative to Marxism, which also addressed the Third World underdevelopment and change. We shall not be concerned with this aspect of modernisation theory here. In a broader sense, it refers to a general view of modernity arising from traditions of classical sociology as expressed in the works of Weber, Marx, Simmel, and the contributions of Ferdinand Töennies, Emile Durkheim, Talcott Parsons, etc. We shall take their theories as a basis for our conceptualisation and will also consider some of the more up-to-date theories. In sum, these contributions can provide a synthetic paradigm, to which the concept of modernity is central and which is essential for the endeavours to understand the driving forces of today's world.

The differences in development of different parts of the globe that, according to Braudel, became marked in the course of the sixteenth century, point to a major discontinuity that occurred at that time. This discontinuity did not find reflection in social sciences until relatively recently, because the dominant approach adopted in them was that of evolutionism. According to it, history can be told as a story, as a "grand narrative" that imposes an orderly picture on the clutter of human events. Even

---

9   F. Braudel: *Civilisation and Capitalism*, Fontana Press 1985.

those theories that noted the breaches of continuity in points of transition, like that of Marx, see history as having an overall direction, governed by general dynamic principles.

The writers who stress the discontinuity of history, such as Anthony Giddens,[10] accentuate the particular discontinuity, or set of discontinuities, associated with the modern period. Modernity, says Giddens, marks a totally new order, completely different from the traditional one. The modes of life brought forth by modernity placed us in the conditions that are unthinkable in all traditional types of social order. The changes involved in modernity are unprecedented both in scope and in content. In terms of scale of changes, they have established the forms of social interconnection that encircled the whole globe; in terms of their intensity they altered even the most intimate and personal features of our everyday existence, created powerful new technology, and produced modern institutions.

The first investigators of modernity were the classical founders of sociology. For Weber, the most important driving force of modernity was what he called "rationalisation" or the spread of rational thinking and rational techniques through all sectors of society. The origins of rationalisation are to be found, according to Weber, in Judaism and Christianity (the replacement in ancient Israel of magical faith by faith in a God with high moral demands) and its powerful expression is to be seen in the formation of the ethics of Protestantism, which lay at the foundation of modern capitalism.

Marx saw a single, overriding transformative force shaping the modern world in capitalism. With the onset of capitalism, the agrarian production in the local manor is replaced by production for national and international markets, which involves commodification, not only of an indefinite variety of goods, but also of human labour. The social order thus created is *capitalistic*

---

10 A. Giddens, *The Nation-State and Violence*, Cambridge, Eng.: Polity, 1985.

in both its economic system and its other institutions. The dynamism of it is explained by the investment-profit-investment cycle that, in the situation when the rate of profit tends to decline, causes the system constantly to expand.

Durkheim disagreed with Marx as to the main driving force of modernity. For him, modern institutions were shaped by the impact of *industrialism*. He saw the influence of capitalist competition on emerging social order as marginal. The main changes, in his view, were produced by the dynamic impulse of a complex division of labour, subjecting production to human needs through the industrial exploitation of nature.

Other sociologists described the problem of modernity in their own ways. Georg Simmel used his concept of "abstraction" to address the same phenomenon as Weber's "rationalisation." The modern world (not the least because of the emergence of the money economy) has grown increasingly abstract as compared to the concrete and personal relations of pre-modern societies. Ferdinand Töennies, a contemporary to both Weber and Simmel used a dichotomy, *Gemeinschaft and Gesellschaft*, to differentiate a modern society (*Gesellschaft*) in which people relate to each other in particular roles, partially defined by contractual arrangements, from a *Gemeinschaft*, community, characterised by a sense of undifferentiated belongingness in a particular group of people. Tönnies argued that modernity consists in a massive shift from *Gemeinschaft* to *Gesellschaft*. Very much the same transformation was meant by Emile Durkheim when he spoke of the shift from "mechanical solidarity" to "organic solidarity." This shift, in Durkheim's view, entailed costs for human individuals in that it brought with it the feeling of having no roots, no firm values, no sense of belongingness, and the state that he called *anomie*. Finally, an American sociologist, Talcott Parsons, in a set of writings about modernity, brings about the category of "differentiation," the institutionalisation in modern society of different functions of what was one institution in pre-modern society (for example the "functions" of kinship grow into separate social, economic, and political institutions).

Among other classical analysts of modernity, two names should be mentioned as having contributed the most to our understanding of its economic aspect—Schumpeter and Hayek. The former is renowned for his acute analysis of the relations between capitalism, socialism, and democracy, and his theory of the economic role of entrepreneurship, while the latter contributed to the study of the role of economic liberalism in creating the preconditions of a "free society."

Thus "modernisation theory" as it is treated in this work is based on the concept of modernity worked out in classical sociology and developed further in writings about capitalism, industrialism, modern technology, liberal political institutions, and human individualism. As capitalism developed historically, it appeared in aggregation with other aspects of modernity. The technological power it brought into the world since the Industrial Revolution was immense. The economy based on production for market exchange opened up unending opportunities for human inventiveness in engineering and entrepreneurship.[11] The information about prices provided by the market served as necessary guidelines for those who were intent on improving their economic lot, i.e., entrepreneurs. This quantum leap in productivity may be said to be intrinsically linked with the development of capitalism.

Advanced industrial capitalism is also accountable for increased well-being of large masses of people on the scale never seen before.[12] The improvement of living standards occurred gradually, but was steady and unquestionable. The Industrial Revolution in all western capitalist countries first brought sharp polarisation to the extremely rich and extremely poor. This trend

---

11   See M. Friedman and R. Friedman, *Free to Choose*, New York 1980.

12   See P. Berger, *The Capitalist Revolution,* New York 1986.

was long-lasting and proceeded with differences in degree and timing in different countries. The peak of inequality in most countries is believed to have been reached just before World War I. After the war, a pronounced levelling of status occurred. Since the 1950's, the situation has generally been stable with inequality neither increasing, nor decreasing. This phenomenon was noticed by Simon Kuznets and is known as Kuznets curve.[13] Modern capitalism, thus, is characterised by greater material well-being and greater material equality than other "modes of production."

With the onset of capitalism, the social structure changed as well. The Industrial Revolution gave birth to a new social stratum—the industrial working class. It brought changes to the occupational stratification of the middle class and the old aristocracy was gradually replaced by the new bourgeoisie. Together with the growth of material production, there occurred a significant change in class representation. The middle strata increased dramatically. This was caused by a technological factor, a smaller labour force was needed for actual production and more for administration; and by a social factor, as business enterprises grew, they become more bureaucratised. There was also a boost in the development of the service sector of the economy that led to a massive shift in the labour force to service occupations and subsequently to the emergence of yet another stratum, the so-called knowledge class.[14]

The emergence of new classes was matched by an unprecedented increase in social mobility. This is closely connected, among other things, with the growth of industrialism, which opened new opportunities; the growth of democracy, which makes sure that these opportunities are available to

---

13   S. Kuznets, 'Economic Growth and Income Inequality', *American Economic Review,* XLV (1955), 1

14   See F. Machlup, *The Production and Distribution of Knowledge in the United States,* Princeton 1962.

all; and the spread of education, which has become the main vehicle of upward mobility. Thus, through the interaction of economic and political forces, modern western societies have gradually removed traditional barriers to social advancement of individuals, and become more "open" in their stratification systems.

Another important feature of modern capitalism is the development of democratic institutions, which puts the activities of government under intense public scrutiny, and guarantees the citizens political liberties, such as free vote, freedom of speech, freedom of association, etc. This presupposes that the political institutions of society are clearly differentiated from the other institutions and are not allowed to merge with them. Thereupon is based the classical distinction between the state and "civil society." If we take a close look on the manner in which modern capitalism and modern democracy developed historically, the above fact may appear as a major paradox: Capitalism grew together with an unprecedented concentration of political power, yet it is associated with the most severe efforts to limit this power. Considering the contemporary world empirically, we may propose that while some capitalist societies are not democratic, all democracies are capitalist. The term "socialist democracy" has proved to be a contradiction in terms.

Modernity, as expressed in modern capitalism, is indispensable from human individualism. The concept of individualism sees a human being as "discovering himself," as being distinct from his family or the community into which he was born. The experience of this discovery makes him feel and act as a free *autonomous individual*. Adam Smith saw the virtue of capitalism precisely in its link with human freedom. The critics of capitalist modernity, from the right as well as from the left, were quite right in stating that this escape from collective solidarities has been very costly. The cost is what Marx called "alienation" and Durkheim "anomie."

To sum up, capitalism, as an expression of modernity, is characterised by a quantum leap in technological development, the increased well-being of the great majority of people, the growth of new, highly mobile classes, a new political system in the form of modern state and institutions of democracy, and a new culture with an emphasis on the individual.

Pre-modern society

Various terms are used to designate the type of society that preceded the modern society: traditional, peasant, status, preindustrial, agrarian, *ancien régime*, etc. They all define the reality of basically the same order, although each of them stresses a different aspect or aspects of it.

The term "traditional" is perhaps the most general of all the terms mentioned and is best suitable to be juxtaposed to the term "modern." Tradition, defined in the simplest way, is justification of action in terms of the past. In traditional cultures, the past is held in esteem and symbols are valued because they express and perpetuate the experience of generations. Tradition is a mode of handling time and space whereby any given experience is inserted into the continuity of past, present, and future, which, in turn, are structured by recurrent social practices. Tradition is not wholly static, since it has to be reinvented by every new generation that receives its cultural inheritance from those preceding it. The full meaning of tradition cannot be understood within the context of traditional culture alone. It is no accident that in oral cultures, which are regarded as the most traditional of all, tradition is not known as such. The invention of writing changed the time-space perception and created a perspective of past, present, and future in which knowledge could be set off from designated tradition. However, in pre-modern civilisations, such reflexivity is still weighing heavily on the side of the past, and is directed to reinterpretation and clarification of tradition. Moreover, since literacy is the privilege only of the few, the daily life remains bound up with tradition in the old sense. It needs radical intervention of reflexivity, as it happened with the coming of modernity, to change the very basis of system reproduction. Thought and action are constantly adjusted to one another, making our daily life intrinsically independent from the past. In the modern situation, the past experience is of value only if it coincides with what can be justified in the light of our present-day knowledge.

Therefore, traditional society is a general concept of the way of organising action and experience, in which references to the past are of utmost importance. The term "status society" is more specific and lays emphasis on the mode of social stratification. Status-based division precedes the modern stratification by class. According to Max Weber, "in contrast to the purely economically determined class situation we wish to designate a status situation every typical component of the life of man that is determined by a specific, positive or negative social estimation of honour [...]. In content, status honour is normally expressed by the fact that above all else a specific style of life is expected from all those who wish to belong to the circle [...]. Specific status honour always rests upon distance and exclusiveness."[15]

Unlike status groups, classes are not communities. "They merely represent possible and frequent bases for communal action."[16] We can speak of classes, when we mean groups of people, united by common economic interest, who operate in the condition of the market.

The principles of formation of classes and status groups are diametrically opposite. The existence of the market excludes all personal distinctions: "Functional" interests dominate. "The status order means precisely the reverse, viz.: Stratification in terms of honour and the styles of life peculiar to status groups as such. If mere economic acquisition and naked economic power

---

15   M. Weber, *Economy and Society*, New York 1968.
16   Ibidem, p. 189.

still bearing the stigma of its extra-status origin could bestow upon anyone who has won it the same honour as those who are interested in status by virtue of style of life claim for themselves, the status order would be threatened at its very root."[17]

The general type of status society as described by Kenneth Jowitt[18] possesses the following characteristics: (*a*) the basic unit of social identification and organisation is the *corporate group*. It is exclusive in its membership and suspicious of other corporate groups, which are regarded as strangers; (*b*) the intra- as well as inter-group relationships are governed by personal—not impersonal—norms of action; (*c*) the division of labour is categorical and stereotypical, and is carried out according to caste, ethnicity, occupational group, etc.; (*d*) such social organisation and division of labour generates in a status society an ontology, "that stresses the concrete and discrete—i.e., discontinuous quality of social reality"[19]; (*e*) the vision of the reality as an indivisible unit commands the perception of economic, social, cultural and political resources as being immobile and finite, rather than expanding and flexible.

Moving in our analysis from status society to "peasant society," we encounter a type in which, not only social, but also economic and cultural features are prominent. The advantage of operating with such a concept is that here we have a concrete human type that has existed throughout history and in different parts of the globe. "Peasant society and culture has something generic about it. It is a kind of arrangement of humanity with some similarities all over the world."[20] We can discern four main classical conceptualisations of peasantry both as a pragmatic generalisation and a specific worldwide type of social structure.

---

17 M. Weber, *Essays in Sociology*, New York 1946.
18 K. Jowitt, *The Leninist Response to National Dependency*, Berkeley 1976.
19 Ibidem, p. 8.
20 R. Redfield, *Peasant Society and Culture*, Chicago 1956.

The Marxist tradition of class analysis has addressed peasantry in terms of power relationships. Peasants appear as the suppressed and exploited producers of pre-capitalist society. In Marx's analyses that were concerned mainly with the classes of the emerging capitalism, peasants were brushed off disdainfully as the "sack of potatoes." The second approach, which can also be traced to Marx, but was first made explicit by Vasilchikov and fully developed by Chayanov, views peasant social structure as being determined by a specific type of economy with the family farm at the centre. The third tradition, which stems from European ethnography and from traditional western anthropology, sees peasantry as representing an earlier cultural tradition and thus as a "cultural lag." The fourth tradition divides societies into the "traditional" (composed of closed and uniform units) and the modern or "organic," based on a division of labour and interaction of units. It can be traced back to Durkheim, but also to Tönnies and Maine.

More recent studies of peasant societies include the works of the scholars of East-European origin—Shanin, Galeski, Thomas and Znaniecki, and also Redfield, Wolf, Thorner, etc.

The common-sense meaning of the word "peasant" is "one who lives in the country and works on land, either as a small farmer or as a labourer."[21] In this sense, it means little more than "non-industrial." Thus, we can differentiate between "industrial" and "peasant" nations. Daniel Thorner suggests that "peasant" societies are those in which half the population is agricultural and more than half the working population is engaged in agriculture.[22] This definition is also very close to the one given by Firth: "By a peasant economy one means a system of small-scale producers, with a simple technology

---

21   *The Oxford English Dictionary.*
22   D. Thorner, *Peasant Economy as a Category in Economic History,* 1961.

and equipment often relying primarily for their subsistence on what they themselves produce. The primary means of livelihood of the peasant is cultivation of the soil."[23]

Such definitions put the main emphasis on the size of landholding and the technology, and say nothing about the operational unit of production and consumption. They also serve as a basis for lumping together all agricultural societies, tribal as well as peasant. In a further search for definitions, Kroeber and Redfield stated that peasants formed a "part society."[24] They maintain that the culture of the peasant community is not autonomous. It is but an aspect of the civilisation. Thus, peasant society is a half-society, and peasant culture is a half-culture.

Thorner elaborated on this by stating that a peasantry can only exist where there is a state, i.e., a hierarchy, or external political power that exercises sovereignty over the particular community of "peasants." There should also be towns with markets, the culture of which is different from the culture of the countryside. Wolf agrees with this when he writes that "the State is the decisive criterion of civilisation . . . which marks the threshold of transition between food gatherers in general and peasants."[25]

An important contribution to the conceptualisation of the peasantry was the emphasis on the basic unit of ownership, production, and consumption. This is what Daniel Thorner added to the definition of peasantry: "In our concept of peasant economy the typical and most representative units of production are peasant family households. We define a peasant family household as a socio-economic unit that grows crops primarily

---

23   Quoted in George Dalton, 'Peasantries in Anthropology and History', *Current Anthropology*, 13, No. 3-4 (June-October 1972).

24   R. Redfield, *Peasant Society and Culture*, Chicago 1960.

25   E. Wolf, *Peasants*, New Jersey 1966, pg. 11.

by the physical efforts of the members of the family. The primary activity of the peasant households is the cultivation of their own land strips or allotments."[26]

Teodor Shanin stresses the fact that there is no division between social and economic spheres.[27] The peasant household is the basic unit of both peasant society and economy. It is characterised by the almost complete integration of the peasant family with the farming enterprise. It also offers socialisation, moral support, and economic help for all family members.

The definition of peasantry offered by Teodor Shanin is as follows: "Peasants can be defined as small producers on land who, with the help of simple equipment and the labour of their families, produce mainly for their own consumption and for meeting obligations to the fields of political and economic power. A wider definition would consider and extend those features: the functioning of the family production unit, traditional agriculture as the main occupation, the life of small rural communities, the specific relations and political economy attached to the under-dog position in society."[28] Let us elaborate on these additional features.

It is the family that provides the labour on the farm. The farm, and nearly only the farm, provides for the consumption needs of the family. Economic action is blended into the structure of family relations and the maximisation of profit does not appear in an explicit form. The family farm also acts as the main unit of property, production, consumption, and socialisation.

---

26 Quoted from T. Shanin, *Peasants and Peasant Societies*, Oxford 1971.

27 T. Shanin, 'The Nature and Logic of the Peasant Economy', *Journal of Peasant Studies*, vol.1, No.1 (Oct.1973).

28 T. Shanin: *Russia as a Developing Society*, The Macmillan Press Ltd., 1985.

Traditional farming is carried out on a relatively low level of specialisation. Food production renders the family farm comparatively self-sufficient. The impact of nature is particularly important for the unit's livelihood.

The way of life of small communities produces a specific traditional culture, characterised by traditional and conformist attitudes, i.e., the justification of individual action in terms of past experience and the will of the community, formal egalitarianism, with high normative value placed on land holding and on the family.

Peasants, as a rule, were kept at a distance from the social sources of power. This political subjugation, together with cultural subordination and economic exploitation through tax, rent, interest, and terms of trade, put them in the position of society slaves.

Now that we have constructed the two oppositely different ideal types, they may serve as two extreme poles, which of course do not exist empirically. One pole represents a pure traditional peasant society, made up of corporate groups, the majority of them peasants, living in isolation from the outsiders, and dependent in their day-to-day life on natural cycles, reflected also in a characteristic epistemology of cyclicity. The technology in such a society will be developed only to the extent that it can serve the satisfaction of the most basic needs. The relationships inside the groups as well as between them will be regulated by personal rather than impersonal norms, collective patterns of behaviour will predominate, and social and geographical mobility will be very low.

On the opposite pole, we find a modern society that is dynamic, composed of role-playing individuals, guided in their relations by impersonal formal rules, who perceive the world in terms of ever-changing opportunity. Such a society will be predominantly divided into classes with strong economic and political interests represented in the institutions of democracy. The economy will be based on highly developed technology and aimed at satisfying ever-growing needs of the consumer. The rates of mobility, both social and geographical, will be very high.

The diffusion of modernity

Before we proceed to the analysis of Russian society with the help of these theoretical constructs, let us consider the ways in which transition from a traditional to modern society takes place. This process is what we shall call in this work "modernisation." Modernity is closely connected with a change in the perception of time and space. The invention of the mechanical clock and its diffusion to virtually all members of the population (an occurrence that dates back to the late eighteenth century) meant the beginning of the process of separation of time from space. Before that, the time of day could not be perceived without reference to other socio-spatial markers: "When" was universally either connected to "where" or identified with natural phenomena. The clock brought with it a uniform dimension of "empty" time, allowing for designation of "zones" of the day. Gradually this uniformity of time measurement was matched by the uniformity in the social organisation of time. An important role in that was played by the worldwide standardisation of calendars. Now we all follow the same dating system: the approach of the "year 2015" thus is a global event.

With the "emptying of time" came the "emptying of space." According to Anthony Giddens,[29] the development of empty space is understood as the separation of *space* from *place*. "Place" can be conceptualised as the physical settings of social activity. In pre-modern societies space and place largely coincide, since geographical locations of social life are always filled with localised activities and are dominated by "presence." The separation of time and space and their "emptying" are responsible for what Giddens calls "disembedding," the lifting out

---

29   A. Giddens, *The Consequences of Modernity*, Stanford 1990.

of social relations from local contexts and their recombination in different locales across indefinite time spans. This process helps to explain why and in what way various influences converge at a particular place. Modern institutions, attitudes, and outlooks are disembedded and can float freely across time and space to be ultimately embedded in different places and under different conditions. They can combine with pre-modern institutions and outlooks thus forming new structures. It is our overall thesis, that Russia, as it modernised, became an aggregate of different modern and traditional trends. Like other countries placed at the periphery of Europe, she received the institutions that originated in the core and the spread of which was caused by the globalising dynamic inherent in modernisation. These new institutions and outlooks were blended with old traditional structures making the Russian social scene immensely complex and equivocal. We shall try to throw some light on these ambiguities and explain the meaning and origin of what are thought to be peculiarly Russian institutions.

***

Part Two: Interpenetration of epochs

Chapter Three

The Responses to the Challenges of Modernity

The political scene

Nikolai Danilevsky, whom we mentioned at the beginning, was not the only one who placed his hopes in the Russian potential to create a new civilisation by pursuing her own chosen way. Similar thoughts were expressed even by Piotr Chaadaev (although somewhat hypocritically) after the boom created by the publication of his *Lettre philosophique*.[30] Various shades of similar thinking were present in the writings of the Slavophiles. The theme of the Slavs as "new barbarians" coming to take initiative from the old European nations was a key note of the lectures delivered in Paris by a young Polish poet, Adam Mickiewicz, whose views, according to Andrzej Walicki, influenced Herzen and other Russian nineteenth century liberals.[31]

However, not only Slavic thinkers held such views. High expectations of the Russian potential were expressed by Friedrich Nietzsche, Oswald Spengler, and indeed Max Weber. The latter belonged to the generation that came after the romantics like Danilevsky. Weber had lived through and closely followed the events of the Revolutions of 1905 and 1917, the fall of the monarchy, and the advent of the Bolsheviks, which in a sense,

---

30   See P. Chaadeav, *Izbrannyje sotchinenia i pisma*, Moskva 1991.
31   See A. Walicki, *Aleksander Herzen. Kwestia polska i geneza pewnych stereotypów*, Warszawa 1991.

gave testimony to the realisation of the hopes of the Russian thinker. His and other writers' evaluations of these events will help us to throw some light on the matter of Russia's identity.

The observers of the Russian social and political scene at the turn of the twentieth century reveal the pervasive sense of ambiguity and duplicity of what was happening. Thus, Weber called the events following the Revolution of 1905 the transition to *Scheinkonstitutionalismus,*[32] a sham or pseudo-constitutionalism, and the aftermath of the March 1917 Revolution, the transition to *Scheindemokratie,*[33] or to pseudo-democracy.

The debate among Russian Marxists as to the nature of the Russian rural economy of the turn of the twentieth century, as summed up by Shanin,[34] placed it between feudalism and capitalism, with definitions like "seem-feudal" or "seem-capitalist" used to pin it down. Discussions are still going on about the Russian *kulak*—was he a traditional peasant type or a modern farmer? The same ambiguity relates to the nature of Russian and Soviet bureaucracy—was it more of a modern civil servant bureaucracy or more of a traditional, patrimonial one? Another ambiguity was placed by Kenneth Jowitt at the root of his conceptualisation of the Soviet partocracy that he characterised as "charismatic impersonality."[35]

Let us look at some of these conceptualisations. Max Weber was fully aware of the dangers the process of *disenchantment* (*Entzauberung*) had in stock for the western civilisation. He was frightened by the prospect of reason—once the liberator

---

32   M. Weber, 'Russlands Ubergang zum Scheinkonstitutionalismus', *Beilage, Archiv für Socialwissenschaft und Socialpolitik,* 1906, no 1.

33   M. Weber, 'Russlands Ubergang zur Scheidemokratie', *Gesamelte Politische Schrifte,* München 1921, pp. 107-125.

34   T. Shanin, *Russia as a Developing Society,* The Macmillan Press Ltd., 1985.

35   K. Jowitt, *The Leninist Response to National Development,* Berkeley 1976.

of man from the bonds of ignorance—becoming man's new enslaver. He thus turned to Russia, because Russia appeared to him as a country unburdened by the experience, fraught with such consequences. As a nation whose culture was only in a formative stage, she could bypass the obstacles that, in Weber's opinion, blocked the road to freedom to European civilisation. As he watched the development of the "Russian drama," his attention focused on the values of Russian liberalism and on the support it received from the economically ascendant interest groups.

The events of the 1905 Revolution demonstrated that such support was not forthcoming. The liberal forces as represented by the *Zemstvo* officials, who were genuinely interested in the reforms, were not joined by the industrial and financial bourgeoisie, who sided with the crown and bureaucracy. As a result, the concessions granted by the tsar's government in the *October Manifesto* did not mean a genuine constitutional system, because it blocked the division of authority between the chief executive and a political party in control of the parliament. It was rather a "pseudo-constitutional" system.

Weber's inquiry had thus brought him to the conclusion that it was a mistake to look at Russia as a bringer of new civilisation. In Russia, as in Europe, the power, he concluded, was passing into the hands of bureaucracy, an event he greatly feared. On the whole, Weber's miscalculation, suggests Richard Pipes,[36] was caused by his assumption that Russia had no political history— that she was a *tabula rasa*—and that her development could be charted in parallels with other, historically "more advanced," countries. Russia, however, did have a history. It was the history of the autocratic state and the history of the vast masses of peasantry, which at the peak of Russian modernisation, i.e., at the start of the twentieth century accounted for "nearly 90

---

36 R. Pipes, 'Max Weber and Russia', *World Politics,* 1955, vol. 7, no 3.

percent of all mass of the population."[37] The modern reforms confronted with traditional patterns of culture and peasant social organisation gave birth to an intermediate *quasi*-structure.

Of interest in our discussion of such ambiguous artificial constructs, obtained as the result of the enmeshment of modern and traditional sociocultural elements, is Kenneth Jowitt's concept of "charismatic impersonality," used to describe the working of the Bolshevik regime in post-revolutionary Russia.

The concept is composed of two mutually exclusive elements—of the Weberian notion of charisma as an affective heroic drive and the notion of impersonality, which lies at the root of modern rational procedural rules. According to Jowitt, charismatic leaders fulfil the mission of combining such fundamentally irreconcilable orientations.

It is their personality, genius, and inspiration that make possible the recasting of mutually exclusive elements into a new unit of personal identity and membership. Jesus Christ, for example, created a new church by recasting the commitment to Judaism as a corporate ethnic identity and the incorporation of the gentile world. Hitler combined ideologically and organisationally two orientations and commitments that were otherwise conflictual—German nationalism with its ethnic exclusivity and "Aryanism" with its pathos of racial supra-ethnicity.

Lenin, Jowitt maintains, "took the fundamentally conflicting notions of individual heroism and organisational impersonalism and recast them in the form of an organisational hero—the Bolshevik party."[38] The obtained amalgam remained conflictual, but its constituent elements were no longer exclusive. Lenin's "party of a new type" combined heroism and impersonality, arbitrariness, and sober empirical calculation. On the charismatic

---

37   Figures from the Russian 1897 national census, quoted in T. Shanin: op. cit., p. 65.

38   K. Jowitt, op. cit., p. 36.

side, the working class, cadres, and Party were called to exercise heroism, to sacrifice in the name of the realisation of historical laws of social development. On the modern side, there was a materialist orientation, rational organisational structure, and rules delimiting the personal authority of the party members.

The charismatic component of Jowitt's conception incorporates also an element that, seemingly, should not be there, namely *tradition*. According to Weber, tradition and charisma are fundamentally antithetical. However, they often merge with one another and sometimes their external forms are similar even to the point of being identical. Their common element is that they put stress on the personal and the substantive, as opposed to the impersonal and the formal.

Noting such a "formal overlap" between charismatic and traditional orientation, Jowitt proceeds to name two more charisma—tradition relationships. First, a charismatic leader gains access to the minds of the members of the society he wishes to transform by possessing, at least in a formal or structural sense, the qualities that are consistent with the features of that society. He is most successful at times of major social turmoil, in a situation of serious disruption and uncertainly, when people are most prone to recommitment. Thus, Christ taught at the time of great turmoil in Israel, and as a rabbi and student of Mosaic law, he was intelligible to his audience and gathered them in large numbers.

Second, the traditional features of a charismatic leader *mediate* between the revolutionary organisation and its need to recruit members from a population that, although ready for recommitment, still retains status or traditional orientations. In his final characterisation of Leninism, Jowitt sees its distinctive quality in the "enmeshment of status (traditional) and class (modern) elements in the framework of an impersonal-charismatic organisation."[39]

---

39   Ibidem, p. 47.

Jowitt's conception of charismatic impersonality, different as it claims to be from Weber's conception of routinisation of charisma, has in the last analysis the same meaning. For Weber, routinisation of charisma meant democratisation of the original doctrine and its adjustment to the needs of those who become the primary carriers of the leader's message. Ultimately, the original ideas either become the guides for the conduct of everyday life of the masses of people, or influence only a small group who remains enclosed in their special way of life and alien to the society at large. "[...] The routinisation of charisma, in quite essential respects, is identical with adjustment to the conditions of the economy, that is, to the continuously effective routines of workaday life."[40] Charisma, thus, has to be contained in the framework of some sort, i.e., institutionalised. The way in which charisma is being institutionalised depends on the organising principle adopted by those who undertake to do it. In the late nineteenth-century Russia, the ground was prepared for the acceptance of both western ideas, and rational (mostly German and Prussian) procedural and organisational conceptions. When they were received in Russia, they underwent filtration through traditional peasant mentalities, and their recombination in Russian condition produced the strange amalgam, termed by Jowitt as charismatic impersonality. The conditions of agrarian economy and peasant sociocultural orientations, predominant in Russia at the turn of the twentieth century, gave modern ideas brought from Western Europe a special traditionalistic twist.

Economic and institutional responses

The economic aspects of Russian modernisation and the particular shape industrialisation took there were perhaps best tackled by Alexander Gerschenkron. In the mid-nineteenth century, the most economically advanced country was England. The second half

---

40   M. Weber, *Wirtschaft und Geselschaft*, vol. I, p. 148.

of the nineteenth century was marked by rapid industrialisation of European countries, such as France and Germany, and starting from the 1880s, of Russia. Whereas England industrialised according to her own logic (and Alan Macfarlane makes a strong case that England was never in her history a peasant society),[41] the latecomers to industrialisation proceeded with her example in mind. Their road to industrialisation, however, was in certain key respects different from that of England. These differences were: the speed of development (the rate of industrial growth), the structures of production and organisation of industry, the role of institutional instruments, the intellectual climate and the "spirit" that accompanied industrialisation, and finally, the degree of backwardness of each individual country and her national industrial potentialities.

Gerschenkron comes to a conclusion that, first, in all the countries mentioned, the initial speed of industrialisation was very high. This was caused mainly by the application of a ready-made superior technology. The only way in which a backward country can achieve success is by application of modern and efficient techniques. This is particularly true because it has to overcome competition from more advanced countries. In the late nineteenth century, Russia concentrated on promotion of those branches of industry in which technological progress was particularly spectacular. She stopped short, however, of indulging in those branches, in which very special technological skills were required. Thus, she didn't turn to the production of machine tools, but launched a large-scale iron and steel production, in which she was highly successful, and in some respects even more innovative than Germany.

Second, industrialisation was carried out on a large scale. The breakthrough in industrialisation could only be possible if it were conducted on a broad front, involving many branches of

---

41 See A. Macfarlane, *The Origins of English Individualism*, Oxford 1978.

economic activities. The reason for that was complementarity and indivisibility in economic processes. It was impossible to start building railroads without having coal mines, steel mills, and the necessary infrastructure. Besides, the scale of industrialisation was prompted by the nature of nineteenth century techniques, which required increases in the average size of plants.

Third, the crucial role in industrialisation was played by the institutions—the banks and the state. In England, which was the first to industrialise, this process went on very gradually, with a considerable accumulation of capital, first from earnings in trade and agriculture and then from industry itself. It didn't necessitate the development of any institutions for long-term financing of industry. Conversely, in more backward countries, like Russia, capital was scarce, industrial activities were broadly distrusted, there was pressure for launching big enterprises to cope with the scale of industrialisation, and last but not least, the entrepreneurial forces were very modest. To cope with these pressures, banks became the main instruments of industrialisation in France, Germany, and the state fulfilled a similar role in Russia.

Fourth, in every case mentioned a special ideology was attached to industrialisation to achieve a breakthrough from backwardness. It turned out that to ignite the imagination of men, to mobilise them to fulfil the tasks of economic growth, material incentives were not enough. Even the businessman and daring entrepreneur should have better legitimisation of their pursuits than high profits. To enter into a new age, to move the mountains of the routine, what is needed is faith—faith in a better future and a more just and equitable world order. What was enough for industrialisation in England, i.e., rational argument and incontrovertible logic, was not enough in the countries that went in her footsteps. In backward countries, ideology and quasi-religious fervour served as a stimulant and a precondition of industrial transformation—socialism in France, nationalism in Germany, and Marxism in Russia.

In Russia, the great wave of industrialisation came in the mid-1880s, that is, almost three decades later than in Germany. The level of the economic development of Russia at the starting point was considerably lower than that of Germany or Austria. "[...] The scarcity of capital in Russia was such that no banking system could conceivably succeed in attracting sufficient funds to finance a large scale industrialisation; the standards of honesty in business were so disastrously low, the general distrust of the public so great, that no bank could have hoped to attract even such small capital funds as were available, and no bank could have successfully engaged in long-term credit policies in the economy where fraudulent bankruptcy had been almost elevated to the rank of a general business practice."[42]

In these conditions, the role of the state in economic transformation was particularly strong. The Russian state was a gigantic enterprise, *sensu stricto,* and at the same time a powerful system of political and administrative intervention, penetrating every aspect of Russia's economy. However, after the revolutionary years of 1905-1906, the role of the state diminished, but was not replaced by independent economic mechanisms, as was the case with Germany. The challenge of industrialisation at that "stage of backwardness" was met by an extremist political organisation equipped with Marxism, which ultimately established a regime, which acted among other things in the name of industrial progress and economic well-being.

---

42 A. Gerschenkron, *Economic Backwardness. Historical Perspective,* Cambridge 1962.

Chapter Four

The Golden Age of Russian Literature

There are several reasons, why we think we are justified in referring to Russian literature for documental proof of our thesis that modernisation has produced in Russia complex and often ambiguous meanings and substances by bringing together attitudes, mentalities, and institutions that represented different epochs. The main reason is our belief that all social sciences and humanities treat the same subject—the human being and the conditions that surround him. As such, they are inseparable, and separation, which has always been artificial, has always had to be compensated for and rectified by broader methodological approaches or interdisciplinary ventures.

Literary study is closely connected with sociology, history, psychology, etc., because they are all centrally concerned with the study of culture, although the word "culture" often means very different things to them. Most literature since ancient times was considered an essential part of the experience of the society—a way of dramatising its myths, celebrating its values, ordering its insights and sensibilities. Since literature is incomprehensible without some real sense of society, it is also true, that "without the literary witness the student of society will be blind to the fullness of a society's life."[43]

---

43 R. Hoggart, 'Literature and Society', in *Speaking to Each Other*, Vol.2, London 1970, pg. 56.

Literature thus is an aspect of society. It reflects, structures, and highlights many of its most profound meanings. In a sense, it is also an institution of society, where there is a complex web of interrelations between writers and audiences, and an inheritance of styles, tastes, artistic practices, and elements of myth and ritual.

It would be a mistake to say that sociology defines social reality, and then a response to it is given in literature. Rather, sociology and literature are both ways in which we shape and structure our sense of what reality is. They are *different* ways of seeing the world. Sociology as a conceptual discipline studies society with particular reference to its institutions and structures. Literature, on the other hand, is a body of written and orally or dramatically transmitted works that itself "interprets" society in its peculiar personal, subjective, and imaginative way.

There are points in history to illuminate which united efforts of sociologists, historians, and lettrists are especially needed. These are the moments of change, the periods of transition and major shake-ups, when, not only conscious ideologies, but also styles, manners, and social structures come under pressure. To assess such changes, literature can be extremely helpful, if not indispensable. It can help not because it is "representative" of general feeling, not because it gives accurate reports of historical events, but because the complex intuition of writers involves them into new relationships with the language they use, the literary structures they create, the sense of function they have, and the audience they secure.

In dealing with Russia, especially with the Russia of the turn of the twentieth century, the question of literature is of particular significance. As we shall try to argue below, in the extremely severe conditions imposed on the society by the Russian autocracy, literature became one of the main channels of political articulation. Accordingly, the role of the writer in Russian society became that of the public tribune, prophet, or messiah. This special role of the writer has been kept up all through the period of the communist rule and up to the present stage of the construction of a democratic state.

Cultural setting

The phenomenon of Russian nineteenth-century literature stands apart in world culture and constitutes the greatest contribution to civilisation that that country has ever made. The traditions it created were to dominate the Russian cultural scene for years to come, its influence in the world was immense, and it was the medium through which Russian national self-identification was made possible.

Russian nineteenth-century literature emerged as a direct consequence of the reforms conducted a century earlier by Tsar Peter I. Its first great representative was Pushkin and it ended with Chekhov; Gorky, who came after him was a transitional case, a cultural link with the new politically-shaped era of "socialist realism."

The cultural life of nineteenth-century Russia was concentrated in St. Petersburg, the offspring of the great tsar-moderniser and the administrative focus of the empire. Up to the present day, this city is unlike any other Russian city and the events that took place there were often regarded as intrusions into the indigenous life of the country. It differs from any other Russian town in climate, layout, architecture, predominant spirit, and mores and lifestyles of the inhabitants. It is as alien to the rest of Russia as New York is to the rest of the United States. The reason for such strangeness in both cases is the same— the convergence of different influences giving birth to a new cosmopolitan culture.

Having been built in a wilderness of northern marshes, away from the traditional centres of Russian life, the nineteenth-century St. Petersburg bears resemblance to the great western cities of that period, bustling with life, tense with contradictions of all sorts, and the scenes of both the greatest human depravity and the highest civic ascension. In Russian culture, this city was reflected as a battlefield of modernity and tradition, the ground on which the great Russian drama was enacted.

A conglomerate on the one hand of trendy constructions, designed and built by the best western architects, and on the other hand, of slums and workers' districts, inhabited mostly by newcomers from villages, this city became a natural breeding ground of contradictions both within the emerging capitalist structure and between the new capitalist and the old peasant mentalities. It was a natural environment for the appearance of a new brand of human being, a modern autonomous individual, dehumanised by the encroaching technical and impersonal civilisation that searched for a new identity in a rapidly changing world.

"The man from underground" is the type of personality that is so characteristic of the St. Petersburg milieu. He is ever present in the novels of Dostoyevsky, appears in the St. Petersburg novels of Gogol, and can be met in the works of most writers connected with St. Petersburg, including contemporary ones, like Andrei Bitov and Iosif Brodsky.

This type of personage makes his appearance for the first time in Pushkin's, *Queen of Spades,* as Herman, the obsessed gambler. Interestingly, this gloomy, maniacal figure stands apart from the rest of Pushkin's characters. It seems that it was the spectre of St. Petersburg itself that cast its dark shadow on the most harmonious of all Russian writers, the "beautiful child" of Russian literature.[44]

---

44 According to Waclaw Lednicki, the tragic perception of St. Petersburg can be traced to a Polish poet Adam Mickiewicz, who described his impressions of the first visit to this city in his poem *Forefathers*. Pushkin was influenced by this perception and developed it first in his *Bronze Horseman* and then in *Queen of Spades*. See W. Lednicki, *Pushkin's Bronze Horseman* (Berkeley and Los Angeles 1955), pp. 50-55.

Dostoyevsky

It is not unnatural for us to begin the review of Russian nineteenth-century literature as a medium in which the workings of modernity and tradition were most graphically reflected, with Fyodor Dostoyevsky, the writer recognised by world scholarship as combining characteristically Russian passions with universal ideas about life and human destiny. It has become a cliché to speak of the modernity of Dostoyevsky and his relevance to our century. The notion of the contemporaneity of his writings has been given constant expression in literature and criticism ever after his death in 1881. His impact on great contemporary writers and thinkers was immense. Dostoyevsky's ideas, images, styles, forms, artistic rhythms can be traced in the works of such a wide variety of writers as Nietzsche, Thomas Mann, Kafka, Gide, Joyce, Faulkner, Henri Miller, Kensaburo Oe, etc. By literary critics he is portrayed as a champion of the "downtrodden and oppressed," a ruthless genius, stylistic innovator, the prophet of a new Christianity, the discoverer of the "man from underground," a spokesman for the values of Eastern Orthodoxy, the herald of the Russian messianic ideas. We shall attempt to unite these approaches in throwing some light on the modern and traditional aspects of his writing.

To begin, Dostoyevsky did not bring any new ideas with him; the ideas expressed by his heroes had already been "in the air" as the author himself so often admitted. What is new in Dostoyevsky, however, is the way in which these ideas are perceived, expressed, lived through. Here we confront the consciousness of an undeniably modern kind. Such consciousness, "the dismantled consciousness" as Mikhail Bakhtin called it,[45] is characteristic both of Dostoyevsky's heroes and of the author's own style of narration. "In the

---

45   See M.M. Bakhtin, 'The Dismantled Consciousness: An Analysis of the 'Double', from Bakhtin's *Problemy poetiki Dostoyevskogo*, Moskva 1963.

confession of the Underground Man," Bakhtin writes in *Problems of Dostoyevsky's Poetics*, "We are struck by an extreme and sharp internal dialogising: there is in it literally not a single monologically firm, undisintegrated word."[46] Such is the "disease of consciousness," to use Dostoyevsky's own characterisation that afflicts the Underground Man:

"Where are my primal causes on which I can rest, where are my foundations? Where can I find them? I exercise myself in thought, and consequently with me every primary cause immediately draws another one after itself, even more primary, and so on into infinity. Such is precisely the essence of all consciousness and thought."[47]

Indeed, such is the essence of all truth or reality in the world of dismantled consciousness—it is always multivalent, because it is perceived by the parts of consciousness that argue with each other. Such a split was a reflection of the complexity of the reality that surrounded the modern man, the reality that produced the Underground Man—a textbook example of Karen Horney's, *Neurotic Personality of Our Time.*[48]

Dostoyevsky exposes the consciousness of the modern autonomous individual in the inner dialogue of his first literary heroes Makar Devushkin in *Poor Folk* and Golyadkin in *The Double* and in the externalised dialogue of the nightmarish talk of Ivan Karamazov with the devil in *Brothers Karamazov*. The use of this new literary technique meant deep-rooted changes in the classical structure of the novel that found their fullest expressions in the literary works of James Joyce. On the whole,

---

46 M.M. Bakhtin, *Problemy poetiki Dostoyevskogo,* Moskva 1963, p. 306.

47 F. Dostoyevsky, *Notes From Underground*, Leningrad 1973, vol. 5, p. 26.

48 See K. Horney *The Neurotic Personality of Our Time*, New Jork 1937.

Dostoyevsky's "polyphonic novel" pre-empted in more than one way many of the great novels of the twentieth century.

Another structural feature of Dostoyevsky's writing is his extensive use of "confession" as a form in which truth is uttered by his heroes. No doubt, Dostoyevsky was influenced by Rousseau's *Confessions*, and a number of parallels can be drawn between the respective works of the two authors: in both Rousseau's *Confessions* and the confessions made by the characters of Dostoyevsky's novels (almost each one of them breaks down with a confession of some sort) some socially-unacceptable, even ugly deeds are admitted; the admissions are made in full awareness of their extraordinariness and originality; the ugly acts are confessed with an underlying conviction of the purifying and liberating effects of such confessions; and most important, these confessions are made by the people who are convinced that there is no authority beyond human conscience legitimate enough to judge human actions.

The latter aspect indicates the value that the two authors attached to human individualism. Both of them took under their protection the average man with his weakness and triviality. Both Rousseau's self-confessions and Dostoyevsky's confessions via his literary personages spelt out the approach of a new era of democracy and human rights, in which the concerns and strivings of the ordinary human being were given the rank of utmost importance. To use de Tocqueville's terms, it was the era of "democracy" coming to replace the era of "aristocracy," or in reference to our above classification, status-based values were giving way to modern class-based attitudes, disregarding the notion of honour in favour of formal and fixed values common to all human beings.

The deeds, confessed by Rousseau and some of Dostoyevsky's heroes are almost identical: "indecent exposure" described by Rousseau and Arkady, the hero of *The Raw Youth*, a petty theft, committed by Rousseau and

Ferdyshchenko in *The Idiot*. The meaning of these deeds to their perpetrators, however, the motives of their confession, and the consequences drawn from such confessions—all these aspects constitute substantial differences between Rousseau's and Dostoyevsky's perception of ethics and morality. To trace these differences would mean throwing additional light on the Russian intellectual outlook of the epoch of the onset of modernity.

First of all, we admit that there is a measure of theatricality and literary coquetry in the confessions of both authors—viewed from the late twentieth-century perspective, this was probably the feature of the genre. Abstracting from this, Rousseau's confessions appear more authentic, more concerned with truth, and the freeing of the individual from the burden weighing on his conscience. Not only does he have the courage to confess, but he takes responsibility for his actions. His courage is based on a rational understanding of human nature and man's weaknesses, generated in Western Europe over the centuries of her history. His sense of responsibility is a product of internalisation of basic human and civil values.

In one of his early episodes, Rousseau describes a deed he had committed forty years earlier: he'd stolen a pink and silver ribbon. When he was caught, he put the blame on the young cook, Marion, saying that she had given it to him. It was the remorse for this deed that made him write his confessions. He writes: "The burden, therefore, has rested until this day on my conscience without any relief; and I can affirm that the desire to some extent to rid myself of it has greatly contributed to my resolution of writing these *Confessions*."[49]

In Dostoyevsky's novel, *The Idiot,* one Ferdyshchenko, a cynical pronouncer of brutal truths, suggests a game at a party at Nastasya Filippovna's—every guest should confess to some bad

---

49 Quoted from R. Feuer Miller *Dostoyevsky and Rousseau: The Morality of Confession Reconsidered*, Englewood Cliff, N.J. 1984.

deed he committed in the past. He himself confesses to having pocketed a three-rouble note left on his hostess's table. When the house maid was accused of the theft, he did nothing to clear her, and moreover, he tried to persuade her to admit the theft. This false accusation of the maid-servant left Ferdyshchenko singularly free from remorse (it even gave him "extraordinary pleasure"). The way in which he confessed the deed, i.e., in a playful manner at a party, suggests that he attached to it a *literary*, rather than moral value.

Other confessions of Dostoyevsky's heroes: Valkovsky, Ivan Karamazov, Stavrogin, the Underground Man, etc., also bear a mark of being a literary gesture, and look more like a parody on the earnest act of Rousseau. Yuri Lotman has observed that for Dostoyevsky "sincerity" often became synonymous in his fiction with self-love, and a confession—a baring of the soul—became self-contemplation, an act of egoism.[50] Dostoyevsky equates Rousseau's solitary vices with his "literary" ones.

The literary motivation of the confessions of Dostoyevsky's characters is essential. The Underground Man feels it to be an important way of "augmenting his style." This is what Robin Feuer Miller says of the motive for confessions of the Underground Man:

"The very act of confession functions as a cathartic atonement; indulgence in the confessional form helps compensate for the content of the confession. He hopes to obtain relief through writing: the act of writing may itself make him a better man. But all his explanations and analyses about the nature of confessions and of their readers cannot bring him closer to the philosophical purpose of a genuine confession—complete honesty, humiliation, or repentance."[51]

---

50   See Y. Lotman, 'Russo: russkaia kul'tura 18-nachala 19 veka', *Zhan Zhak Ruso. Traktaty*, Leningrad 1969, pg. 604.

51   R. Feuer Miller, ibidem, pg. 88-89.

The main difference between Rousseau and the pertinent characters of Dostoyevsky's novels, thus, is that the latter do not know to whom they should confess and why they should do so. They lack the sense of purpose dictated by the internalised religious, civil and social values; they do not take the very act of confession seriously, they play act and parody confession. The value they *do* see in a confession is of a *literary* kind. The confessions of Dostoyevsky's heroes illustrate the emergence in Russia of the modern individualised person who is struggling to be so, yet is unable to shake off socially accumulated ritual and prejudice. He is thus doomed to buffoonery and self-mockery. His efforts to come to terms with his existential being fail to reach beyond the limits of literary gesticulations:

"Valkovsky, the Underground Man, Stavrogin, Totsky seek a kind of moral exoneration through the fact that the event and its retelling resemble the aesthetic contours of fictional art. For all these characters, a life that has come to resemble literature is at the same time absolved from serious moral accountability."[52]

Dostoyevsky has touched upon what is probably one of the most essential features of the uprooted Russian intelligentsia— its preoccupation with literature-inspired ideals and its endemic inability to go beyond literature and see life without its prism. *The Idiot* and *The Possesed*, the two most artistic novels of Dostoyevsky (in contradistinction to his "ideological novels" like *Brothers Karamazov* or *Crime and Punishment*) illustrate this most clearly.

These literary preoccupations formed a part of the outlook of Dostoyevsky's "modern" characters. Indeed, there is a sharp line, dividing all of his main heroes into modern; oriented towards western ideas and lifestyles, rational and cosmopolitan in their outlooks, alienated from their environments; and

---

52   Ibidem, pg. 94.

traditional—adhering to the ideals of Orthodox faith and Slavic ethnicity, advocating *sobornost'* (communalism), and preaching Russian messianism. The confrontation between the two types of outlook is what constitutes the ideological pattern of almost all of Dostoyevsky's works since his breakthrough novel *The Man from Underground*.

The bearers of the modern outlook are Versilov, Stavrogin, Ivan Karamazov, Raskolnikov, Verkhovensky, etc., while the Russian traditional values are upheld by Alesha Karamazov, Prince Myshkin, and Zosima. Among these two types, no one is rigid in his professed ideology. Each one is struggling with doubts, trying to understand the position of his opposite number, and goes through a painful process of crystallisation of his views. This is wherein lies the supreme artistic value of Dostoyevsky's writing—his heroes, although polarised ideologically, maintain their psychological authenticity. Moreover, they appear as the archetypes of Russian intelligentsia spotlighted at the peak of Russia's cultural activity.

The ideology that is a moral winner in the confrontation between the two groups is that of Russian Christianity. However, its advocates find it hard to deal with the realities of life. They are idealists who, while being able to impress the others, are little able to influence the course of events. They seem to be too good to exist in real life. They bear the outlook of the world that possesses a certain primordial harmony, unmarred by rationalism, and untouched by human individualism. This image of the world is juxtaposed to western rationalism and the values of western Christianity. In his attack on western civilisation and on Catholic theocracy, Father Paisy proclaims in *The Brothers Karamazov*:

"The Church is not to be transformed into the State. That is Rome and its dream, and it is the third temptation of the Devil. On the contrary, it is the State that must be transformed into the Church, rise to its level and become a Church over the whole world. That idea is diametrically opposed to ultramontanism and to Rome, and it is the glorious mission of Orthodoxy to bring it about."[53]

Tolstoy

Dostoyevsky's characters are clear-cut St. Petersburg types. Dostoyevsky himself is a *par excellence* St. Petersburg writer. In contrast to him, Leo Tolstoy is a writer of Moscow and thus in a sense is more "Russian." His outlook is more uniform than Dostoyevsky's. He is a bearer of a peasant epistemology, viewing life in general rather than abstract categories. He was mistrustful of science, sceptical of art, and critical of modern "urban" values and lifestyles. The characterisations most often given to him by critics are: prophet and moraliser. His doctrine of moral goodness and non-opposition to evil by violence is peasant and early Christian in nature. It was coloured by a Russian Orthodox understanding of Christian values (although Tolstoy himself constantly argued with the Russian Church and was excommunicated from it by the Holy Synod not long before his death). Tolstoy's teachings exposed the values of Russian *orthodox civilisation* in the sense in which Arnold Toynbee used that concept.[54] His teachings also have a specific "nihilistic" twist common to so many Russian educated men of that epoch. Nikolai Strakhov, a critic and a contemporary of Tolstoy wrote about him:

"Tolstoy's sympathies aspired to *the simple and good*; that this liberated spirit, able to see life not in abstract forms and not from particular points of view, but in all its plenitude and wholeness, stubbornly seeks for genuine life among every kind of false appearances; and that it finds this only in that which

---

53   F. Dostoyevsky, 'Brothers Karamazov', [in:] *Polnoe sobranie sochinienij*, St. Petersburg 1911, vol. 16, pg. 110.

54   See A. Toynbee, *A Study Of History,* London, New York, Toronto 1956, vol. 1.

represents the purest moral beauty, in that which is simple and meek to the point of self-humiliation, and at the same time firm and composed to a level of the highest magnanimity . . . On no writer does the imprint of *the Russian soul* lie so manifestly as on Tolstoy. This is the very form of moral ideas that was inspired in our people by Christianity or, if you will, in which our people has embodied its religious ideas. This spirit lives in us, stifle and deny it as we may, and if it deserted us then Russia would drop like a corpse abandoned by life [all italics Strakhov's]".[55]

Tolstoy as a representative of the Russian Orthodox outlook has, more than others, uncovered the deficiencies of it. His doctrine bears the marks of a mystical and other-worldly nature of Russian Orthodoxy and its difficulty in tackling the realities of the changing world. Within its framework, there wasn't enough room for his massive personality. Thus Tolstoy always remained a half-pagan who robed himself in Christian clothes. He was well aware of it, too.

The ambiguities that we see in Dostoyevsky's characters are also present in the characters of Tolstoy. Levin, in his *Anna Karenina,* undergoes the same painful search for positive religious values as does Ivan Karamazov or any other of Dostoyevsky's "modern" heroes. They are all unable to reconcile within themselves the conflicting epistemologies by stepping onto the ground of faith, or turning to a tradition of ethics created by the church. Russian Christianity failed to create such a tradition. It was too weak and too entangled with the secular rulers of Russia to establish authoritative ethical standards. Hence, its role was taken over by the literary men, intelligentsia, hence, the prophets like Tolstoy and Dostoyevsky, hence, Russian *religious* philosophy.

---

55 N. Strakhov, *Kriticheskie stat'i ob I.S. Turgeneve i L.N. Tolstom,* Moskva 1901, pg. 43.

Tolstoy's outlook is fundamentally patriarchal and peasant-based. This trait didn't escape a shrewd scrutiny from Lenin who remarked to Gorky: "Before this count there was no genuine peasant in literature."[56]

Tolstoy's views are most transparent in his essays on art. In denying modern art, he not only gives preference to human conscience over artistic conscience, as W. D. Howells rightly points out,[57] but reveals his inability to come to terms with modern social values as such. Modern art is too *artificial* for him to be taken for granted. Tolstoy's abnegation of art meant the denial of the values upheld by the role-playing *socialised* individual, it meant his preference of the values of the *Gemeinschaft* over those of the *Gesellschaft*.

Tolstoy understood art as "an activity by means of which one man, having experienced a feeling, intentionally transmits it to others."[58] True works of art, according to Tolstoy, should answer three criteria; they should: (*a*) express an important and useful idea; (*b*) meet the set standards of technical workmanship; (*c*) be a product of an honest feeling. Tolstoy formulates these criteria after having examined the bulk of esthetical theory from Baumgarten to Hegel. The conceptions he doesn't include in his review, as George Bernard Shaw in his essay points out,[59] indicate the bias in his own esthetical outlook. Thus, concentrating on the intentionality of transmission of feeling, he ignores a definition of art as the expression of pleasure in work. Of course, agrees George Bernard Shaw, art is the expression of feeling; "but it

---

56 Quoted from *Leo Tolstoy, A Critical Anthology,* edited by Henry Clifford (Harmondsworth 1971), pg. 129.

57 See W.D. Howells, *The Philosophy Of Tolstoy*, London 1959, pg. 172-74.

58 L. Tolstoy, 'Cto takoe isskustvo' [in:] *Sobranie sochinenij,* Moskva 1964, vol. 15, pg. 87.

59 See G. B. Shaw, 'Tolstoy on Art.' [in:] *Pen Portraits and Reviews*, London 1932.

covers a good deal of art work that, whilst proving the artist's need for expression, does not convince us that the artist wanted to convey his feeling to others. There have been many artists who have taken great pains to express themselves to themselves in works of art, but whose action, as regards the circulation of those works, has very evidently been dictated by love of fame or money rather than by any yearning for emotional intercourse with their fellow-creatures."[60]

Tolstoy's view of art as fulfilling a special mission is another expression of his traditionalistic outlook. In a status-based peasant society, art is seen as a charismatic medium of social mobilisation. Once again, artistic conscience serves as a substitute for political conscience; men of letters in Russia have always fulfilled the role of public tribunes; a "literary public sphere" has always dominated in Russia over a "political public sphere." Even now, in the mid-nineties in post-communist Russia, an average secondary school pupil if asked about the role of art is most likely to answer that art is called to bring forth the ideals of "goodness and peace" and "bring people closer together."

It is no wonder that Tolstoy was unable (and unwilling) to understand Shakespeare, the writer in whom modernity has found one of its first and most powerful advocates. Tolstoy's almost unnatural hate of Shakespeare speaks of his desire to push away all that reminded him of his own natural instincts, his own individualism, which he cursed as his greatest temptation. This individualism of Tolstoy's put him in line with the foremost European writers of his epoch. It is this dawning sense of the uniqueness and the inherent freedom of the human being that Tolstoy shared, together with the other great men of the nineteen's century, that stands behind Tolstoy's psychological insights, his sensitivity to all kinds of human depravity, and his acute social analyses. This modern sensitivity entangled with a

---

60   Ibidem, pg. 257.

patriarchal outlook is what makes Tolstoy such a complex man and such a true representative of the times he lived in.

Russian culture: modern or traditional?

As we have tried to show above, Russian nineteenth-century literature bears testimony to the epoch into which it was born. Similar to Tolstoy's ethical philosophy, Russian philosophy at large, as represented by Soloviev, Shestov, Chomiakov, Berdiaev, Merezhkovsky, etc., did not develop into an exercise in "pure reasoning" like western philosophy. It remained a "religious philosophy," as it was called in Russian intellectual circles, and was closely connected with the two major political-cultural movements of Slavophilism and Occidentalism. Being thus circumscribed ideologically, it generally did not overstep the limits set by either nationalism or traditionalism. An example of the latter is the presence in Russian philosophy of the epistemologically peasant-based concept of natural cyclicity. Thus, Danilevsky divides the process of civilisation into four periods: (*a*) the formative period; (*b*) the building up of cultural and political independence; (*c*) the blossoming; (*d*) the decline and disintegration.[61] Similarly Leontiev sees civilisation as passing through the stages of (*a*) "primary simplicity" (birth, childhood); (*b*) "positive disintegration" (youth, adulthood); (*c*) "simplificatory fusion" or "secondary simplicity" (old age, dying). Such a view of historical process in discrete and self-limiting terms is characteristic, not only of Russian nineteenth-century thinkers, but also of some of the contemporary Russian social analysts.[62]

---

61 N.Y. Danilevsky, *Rossija i Evropa*, Moskva 1869.

62 For example see V.B. Pastukhov, 'Rossijskoje Demokraticheskoe Dvijenie: Put' k vlasti', in *Politicheskie issledovania*, Moskva 1992, no 1, 2.

As we can see, the ambiguity that we have traced in Russian politics is also present in Russian culture. It comes to the fore in the cultural and political division into Westerners and Slavophiles. The latter, as noted by Andrzej Walicki, represents a *Weltanschaung* that constitutes one of the Russian variants of a conservative romantic anti-capitalism.[63] It is rationalised by glorifying the values of Slavic ethnicity and stressing a specific Russian heritage as expressed in Russian Orthodoxy. The line dividing Slavophiles and Westerners sometimes was so thin, that positive identification in many cases became very difficult. Alexander Herzen, for one, combined the two trends in such a manner, that the definitions of his outlook ranged between "revolutionary Slavophilism" and "Russian socialism."

To sum up, the picture of the Russian cultural scene of the period leading up to the Revolution of 1917 was complex and marked by the coexistence of mutually opposing trends. The prevailing impression the observer of it gets is that of transitoriness and anticipation of a final resolution. Russia seems to be on the edge of making a step that will decide her future and resolve a situation tense with expectation, duplicity, and uneasiness.

It seems appropriate at this point to recall the impression of Max Weber who used the Hegelian concept of *Schein* (illusoriness, seemingness) to describe Russian contemporaneous political life.

A similar feeling of the unreality of what was happening was shared by many of the Russian intellectuals. To use a symbol, let us quote one of Dostoyevsky's personages, who one morning is looking at the city of St. Petersburg: "A hundred times over, in such a fog I have been haunted by a strange but persistent fancy: What if this fog should part and float away, would not all

---

63 A. Walicki, Aleksander Hercen. *Kwestia polska i geneza pewnych stereotypów*, Warszawa 1991.

this rotten and slimy town go with it, rise up with the fog and vanish like smoke, and the old Finnish marsh be left as before, and in the mist of it, perhaps, to complete the picture, a bronze horseman on a panting overdriven steed."[64]

---

64   F. Dostoyevsky, 'Raw Youth' in: *Novels of F. Dostoyevsky*, vol. VII, p. 132.

Part Three: Sphinx or no sphinx?

Chapter Five

Social Structure and Cultural Response

Let us now return to the discussion of Russian uniqueness. As we have seen, the time when this question was raised in Russia was marked by the entanglement of discrepant modern and traditional elements in Russian economy, culture, and social structure. We have attempted to analytically disassemble this socio-cultural aggregate. For this we have made use of the ideal types of modern and traditional peasant society. The theory of modernity as we understand it in this work provides us with mechanisms to explain how different trends—cultural, social, political, technological, etc.— came to be aggregated at that point in space and time, and persisted with the acquired dynamic of their own.

We have proposed that the causal force of such a development was a major discontinuity, which occurred with the coming to the fore of the trends that were called modern. We have undertaken to explain what we understand by this term and how this concept was treated in classical and modern sociology. We have established that one of the most meaningful motor forces of modernity was disembedment—the "lifting up" of social relations from local contexts—and their re-embedment in other locations among other types of relations, attitudes, and institutions. This produced complex aggregates, or *ensembles*, as Braudel called them, which were composed of often very different and contradictory elements. There were areas where the process of modernisation was endemic and was subsequently controlled and contained within certain institutions, and behavioural and attitudinal frameworks. The areas located away from these centres of modernisation came under the influence of these trends as coming from without, and, being unable to cope with their dynamics, worked out compromises with them. The evidence we have supplied of such compromises in Russia, suggests that she belonged rather to the second group. We shall presently try to specify her place in this group.

Dependent society

Kenneth Jowitt in his book, *The Leninist Response to National Dependency,* gives several examples of the countries being obsessed with their relation to the West and accordingly with their worth as compared to it. Romania is one example. The other examples are various countries of Eastern and Central Europe, Africa, Asia, and Latin America. In the second half of the nineteenth century in all of these countries, there were elites who made it their vocation to define their attitude to Western Europe and to formulate their countries' respective statuses in relation to her. Usually, their formulations were not much different from those of the Russian elites and were polarised between total admiration of Europe and dignified rejection of her values as inhuman and evil. Jowitt sees in such attitudes the symptom of what he calls national dependency on the west.

According to Jowitt, beginning from the late nineteenth and early twentieth centuries, the countries of Eastern Europe and Latin America closely resembled the Third World in their political organisations and mental attitudes. Jowitt sees three features that constitute this similarity.[65] First, in each of these countries there existed an enormous gap separating the social elite from

---

65   K. Jowitt, *The National Response to National Dependency*, Berkeley 1976.

the peasantry. In Romania, for example, this gap constituted an "abyss," to use Dobrogeanu-Gherea's evaluation. In Russia, where the peasantry was numerically overwhelming and submerged in virtual slavery, the level of social malintegration was terrifying.

Second, there was a mechanical and uncritical transfer of western liberal institutions, irrespective of whether they fitted local conditions or not. Such transfer occurred with a distortion of these institutions' initial meanings, and was reduced to the borrowing of mere institutional facades. The discrepancy between the declared function and operation of the "imported" institutions was striking.

Third, there were multiple (cultural, economic, political, strategic, etc.) dependencies on the West. Here we can point to substantial differences between Russia and the rest of the countries named. The dependencies of Romania or Poland were more pronounced, since these countries were in a direct political orbit of an external power. Russia, on the other hand, was herself an imperial power and exercised influence over smaller states that were her clients. She was, however (and this is probably one of her "unique" features), at the same time heavily dependent on the West culturally and economically.

Jowitt's definition of dependency is as follows: "Dependency is a consequence of the premature, but imperative adoption of a political format for which the appropriate social base is lacking."[66] The imperative nature of such adoption is explained by Jowitt by the need of the weak countries to make themselves intelligible in the eyes of the strong countries to be recognised by them politically. This is necessary to prepare the ground for the subsequent laying of various claims on the strong countries— mostly those of economic aid and military protection. Naturally, such explanation may not apply to Russia, although it may fit some smaller countries very well.

---

66   Ibidem, p. 23.

Further reasons for the adoption of western institutional facades, however, seem to accord with the motives of Russian elites. They are: "the association made by certain elites between particular institutional facades and the elite's presumed ability to effectively centralise a fragmented polity and society, the appropriation of new ideological idioms by unestablished elites with little access to the traditional sources of authority, and the tendency of some elites facing desperate economic and social circumstances to fall back on a quasi magical type of political behaviour."[67] These motives became evident in Russia with gradually increasing clarity as she moved further on the road of modernisation. They were not so evident in the late nineteenth century, as reforms were being conducted by Witte and Stolypin; they appeared under a misleading guise in the Bolshevik initiated communist rule; and they have come to the fore in their explicit and naked form in the post-communist stage of Russian social transformation.

It is worth making a point here that all dependency characteristics that may be applied to Russia may hold only with an eye to a historical perspective. The period of the communist rule constituted a major break in Russian historical continuity, and the exit from it highlights the trends predominant in Russia *before* she plunged into the communist engineered totalitarianism. The way in which she emerges out of it serves as a key to interpreting her standing before the turmoil of 1917. To put it in another way, the trends that had accumulated in Russia by the late nineteenth century were so compulsive and at the same time so dark and incomprehensible to the contemporaries, that the Bolshevik coup appears to be a way of resolving this tension by shutting the front door to these trends and allowing some of them in through the back door and under different names.

It is with this digression in mind that we shall proceed to examine further indications of Russian dependency. Another

---

67   Ibidem, pg. 24.

factor that is responsible for the premature adoption of modern institutions is the peasant and status-based social structure of the countries that adopt them. This structure makes the dependent countries see the world in status terms, i.e., as a hierarchy to which they must conform. Jowitt gives the example of Mongolia, which yielded to the Soviet influence, not only because she sought protection from expanding China, but also, and perhaps mainly, because the outlook predominant there was characteristic of a feudal society, whereby even "independence" was perceived in feudal terms. The Mongolian leaders thought in terms of "dual authority"—over those below and under those above.

We have scarce reasons to believe that this feature of dependency was fully applicable to Russia at the period under discussion. After all, Russia was a great power and played a dominant role in world affairs. She was not the top power in the world, though. The late nineteenth and the beginning of the twentieth century was the time of the unquestionable English hegemony. The view of the world scene was different in Russia as compared to more modern countries. The Russian view was based on evaluation according to status, rather than achievement or impersonal standards. She was a military, but not an economic power in the world. Her heroic and charismatic orientations were soon to give way to rational and economic ones. Thus Russian dependency, in the sense in which it is presently discussed, may be said to have existed in a covert form. The pre-modern nature of her social organisation carried in it the dependency at least in a potential form. This symptom came to full light after the collapse of communism when Russian self-assurance could no longer be sustained by quasi-magical considerations.

Another sense in which a status-based peasant society may be dependent on the outside world is its client relation to world centres, which among other things, prompts a specific understanding of foreign loans and protectionist policies. The share of political economic arguments in explaining this phenomenon may be considerable; at this point, however, we would like to concentrate on the *meaning,* in the eyes of the elites, of what we see as dependent behaviour.

Economic aid, provided by patron states, is perceived in dependent societies as something that is due to them because of their status in the world hierarchy. Foreign loans thus are not viewed in rational economic terms as contractually binding transactions. They are rather seen as free gifts or largesse from their patrons. Jowitt gives examples when a donor's insistence on sticking to the terms of repayment produced perplexity and disgust on the part of some Third World recipients of foreign loans.[68]

Did Russia reveal a similar attitude? Again, we should regard the matter from a perspective. As in the cases analysed above, such a syndrome did exist in Russia in its covert form in the mid- and late-nineteenth century and became fully intelligible when the country found herself in dire need after the collapse of the communist dictatorship. Russia has always received foreign aid in various forms. Depending on the ambitions of the regimes in power, she also was in varying degrees anxious to keep her end of a contract. There was always, however, a ready-made vision of the West as a rich neighbour that by its very status is obliged to share its affluence if it were to act up to its aspirations. The ascribed failures of the West to fulfil this function produced in Russia different reactions that, depending on social and institutional roles of those expressing them, ranged from moral indignation, to a condescending pity, to the attempts at outright blackmail.

The attitude towards economic aid in dependent countries is closely connected with the basically peasant "limited good" view of values and goods. This view is also at the root of their hypersensitivity to the depletion of natural resources. Once again, more is involved here than considerations of political economy. The elites in dependent countries perceive any outside claims on

68   Ibidem, pg. 28.

the natural resources as infringements on their national substance. In this respect, Russia seems to conform to the characteristics of the discussed societal category. The zealousness with which numerous Russian elites at different times guarded any access to their natural resources from the outside is notorious and well documented. The present-day post-communist liberals seem to have gone not much farther than their various predecessors; the difficulty with which legislation on privatisation of resources and participation in it of foreign capital is being passed in Duma is a clear illustration.

Elites in dependent societies, like other strata, are the carriers of the epistemology that makes a clear distinction between those from inside and those from outside. This attitude is a projection of the outlook of a compact peasant community that is isolated from the rest of the world and sees it as potentially hostile. This compact peasant community is the only *moral* community. Those outside are not so much *im*moral as *a*moral.

Such attitude gives the members of peasant societies a convenient right to treat outsiders with omission of the principles that they may otherwise apply in communication inside their own circles. This means that outsiders are not taken for granted, they are not credible, moral norms are not applicable in dealings with them: they may be cheated, manipulated, and fooled without any moral restraints. Such attitude was confirmed as being widespread in Russia by many foreign travellers.[69] The practice of official contacts and negotiations with Russian political and business representatives added more proof of this peculiar idiosyncrasy.

Another feature outlined by Jowitt as being characteristic of dependent societies is their special state organisation. Under conditions of dependency, state functions as an "international diplomatic personage." In that function, it conducts policies

---

69   See G. Kennan, *The Marquis De Custine and His 'Russia in 1839',* Princeton 1970, H. Smith *The Russians*, New York 1976.

with an exceptional anxiety about the reaction they are likely to produce in the outside world. In Russia, this is clearly seen at turning points in her history, when characteristic moves of her elite leaders were directed at pleasing the West more than they were at solving real problems at home. At such points, successes in foreign policies are particularly spectacular while nothing much happens on the domestic front. Among various Russian state leaders even Stalin happened to act in such manner, not to mention Khrushchev or Gorbachev.

To sum up, in comparing Russia with Jowitt's model of dependent society, several conclusions can be drawn. First, in some key respects Russia does conform to this model. She seems to answer the main criterion of dependency, outlined by Jowitt as "pre-modern but imperative adoption of a political format for which the appropriate social conditions are lacking." We are not sure, however, that Jowitt's arguments about the reasons causing a dependent status are fully applicable to Russia, or are exhaustive as applied to any dependent country. Wallerstein's theory of the world system seems to supply an additional perspective to the problem. Apart from this, certain features of dependency formulated by Jowitt, like the elites' striving to become intelligible to the West, the projection on international relations of tendencies active in the traditional social structure, the meaning attached to foreign aid, and the insider-outsider distinction, appear to hold true also in relation to Russia.

Second, Russia's peculiarity within this model can be seen mainly in the fact that she herself was a major geopolitical power, one, however, that was clearly dependent culturally and economically.

Third, the syndrome of Russia's dependence was of a different degree of strength at different points in her history. It may be agreed to have existed in a hidden and initial form at the time of Russia's great nineteenth century identity debate, it acquired a specific institutional guise under communist rule, and it came fully to the fore after total collapse of communism in Russia.

Developing Society

A thesis of Teodor Shanin is that Russia at the turn of the twentieth century revealed the characteristics that later in the fifties served as a basis for formulating the concept of "developing" society.[70] The theoretical grounds on which Shanin came to such a conclusion were not much different from those of Jowitt when the latter spoke of the dependency syndrome. In fact, another way for Shanin to name a developing society is a society that is going through a "dependent development." In our view, Shanin's conceptualisation deserves most serious attention since he is one of the most insightful students of Russia's modernisation.

The meaning that Shanin puts into the concept of developing society is contrary to the vision of development as a unilinear process. It rejects the universality of the road of transition from feudalism to capitalism, holistic analysis of "systems," and the evolutionist solutions, whereby societal forms are steps on the road to some higher society. Instead, it rests on the assumption of the "uneven" and combined development of different societies that presupposes, not only different speeds and times, but also different *roads*, each characterised by its own logic and potential. The societal category of this kind will have a specific social structure, its own type of social reproductions, and its own pattern of social transformations.

The developing societies are placed low in the global hierarchies of power, technology, capital, and science. In the conditions of the free market, the disadvantages arising from such position tend to accumulate as the stronger powers use their upper hand placement in their economic and geopolitical interests.

Internally, the economic scene of the countries of dependent development is fragmented. The key elements of

---

70   T. Shanin, *Russia as a 'Developing Society'*, The Macmillan Press Ltd 1985.

national economy operate within international networks and are controlled by multinational companies. Islands of modern technology brought in from advanced areas of the world are interspersed among outdated production techniques and mass underemployment. There is a sharp division between "modern" industries and finance on the one hand and primitive agriculture, peasant-in-town groups, and "informal economy" on the other. The state is omnipresent, not only as a political, but also as an economic power structure; the role it plays is described as "state capitalist." This means that its functions, besides the control of the instruments of repression, include the supervision of production processes, the casting of roles in administrative and economic bureaucracies, the distribution of social privileges, and the direct control of foreign trade, of mass media, etc.

The control of the industry and finance in the developing societies lies, according to Shanin, in the hands of a "triple alliance" of international capital, state technocrats, and local bourgeoisie. The first two parties of this alliance are the most powerful, while the third is servile, but not at all weak. The working compromise of those forces determine the manner in which a dependent economy is run: The capital is in the state of constant shifts and confrontations in search of quick profits, while the state enterprises are the main instrument of long-term investment and capital accumulation. The large plebeian masses are excluded from economic gains of "dependent development," which breeds extreme social polarisation with inherent social tension.

"Dependent development" in Shanin's terms is "a process of social reproduction of extensive and extending inequality on both an international and local scale. The consistency of the international 'gap' is the expression of its fundamental 'laws of motion' while many more localised 'gaps' and disarticulations follow similar patterns. So do the patterns of repression, the typical cognition of social reality and the ideologies of its change."[71]

---

71 Ibidem, pg. 185.

At the beginning of the present work, we made a brief mention of different approaches to Russian history and various interpretations of her transformation. Broadly speaking, these approaches were dominated either by the deterministic vision informed by what can be reduced to the concept of "Asiatic despotism," or were the attempts to explain the dramatic and grotesque reality of "socialist experiment." Even before this socialist experiment came to an embarrassing end, there appeared attempts to place Russia in a new theoretical perspective. The events of the post-communist Russian transformation proved that the debate about the nature of the developing societies can be most illuminating also in respect to Russia. According to Shanin, at the turn of the twentieth century, "Russia was a country with a massive peasant population, a per capita annual income of less than one hundred dollars, a major presence of foreign capital, and a government pursuing industrialisation policies in a world increasingly dominated by 'the West', that is, the main capitalist industrial societies."[72] Clearly, this picture is highly reminiscent of the societies we came to term as "developing."

Shanin goes on to elaborate that, arguably, Russia was the first developing society ever to emerge on the face of the Earth. The above characteristics of this societal category came to be present there by the close of the nineteenth century. The dependence on foreign capital was there and growing. Estimates show that by 1914, 43 percent of the shareholding capital in Russian industrial, banking, and trading private enterprises was foreign.[73] Foreign capital owned up to two-thirds of Russia's private banks, mines, and manufacturing enterprises.[74] The road

---

72 Ibidem, pg. 186.

73 L. Eventov, *Inostrannye kapitaly v russkoi promyshlennosti*, Moskva 1931, pp. 37-41.

74 P.A. Khromov, *Ocherki ekonomicheskogo razvitia Rossii,* Moskva 1967, pp. 134 and 144-8, quoted in Shanin's ibidem.

predicted for Russia if she continued to go this way was that of "becoming a semi-colonial possession of European capital."[75]

Also present in Russia at the time was the "triple alliance" of capitals—the foreign, the state, and the local. State planners were viewing industrial development as coterminous with modernisation and westernisation. Most of the major enterprises were incorporated into international economic circuits and had little relation to the domestic economy. The level of technological innovation was extremely low, with some of the largest factories using unqualified peasant labour and often pre-mechanical traditional crafts. The polarisation within the economy was matched by social polarisation between the social "top" and the poor strata of the city and the village. The political tension in these conditions was building up as the resentment of the popular masses grew and the intelligentsia was becoming more articulate in their ideological and ethical protest.

The picture of Russia as a country that has revealed the symptom of a developing society was drawn by Shanin with full awareness of the features that also distinguished her from the countries that later came to constitute the Third World. First of all, she was a European (Eurasian) power of considerable magnitude of military, economic, and intellectual potential, which participated in the world politics on an equal footing with other major European powers. Shanin suggests the following classification. First, there was a group of countries that benefited from the early development of capitalism in its mercantile, industrial, and colonial form. It was opposed to the group of countries that were either the direct victims of such development of capitalism (often the colonies of the countries mentioned), or were the regions that the modernity did not favour with its visit at all. Russia, however, belonged to a third intermediate group, made of the countries that reached the threshold of a large-scale

---

75 D. Mirsky, *Russia, A Social History,* London 1952, p. 269. quoted in Shanin's ibidem.

industrialisation later than those of the first group, but avoided the disruptive effect of foreign conquest or colonialism.

The foremost in this group was the United States of America. Her case, however, was special and will not be discussed here. The main core of the third group was Germany, Japan, and Russia, the last being clearly behind the first two in terms of her social, economic, and political achievement. The policies adopted by these three countries in their attempts to catch up with the first group and break through what we would call today "dependency" or "development of underdevelopment" envisaged the powerful role of the state, intervening to speed up industrialisation. Germany's successes in these policies already became visible in the late nineteenth century, while we had to wait until the middle of the twentieth century to see Japan's spectacular rise to world's pre-eminence. Russia's transformation was more painstaking and followed a more crooked path.

Shanin distinguishes between three stages of Russia's modernisation at the turn of the twentieth century. The first stage was initiated by Witte and was conducted along the lines of the reforms theorised by Friedrich List and accepted by the whole middle group of the aspirants to the capitalist development. In Germany, these reforms were conducted by the extremely interventionist state that did all to protect German industry and allow it to "mature," while at the same time undertaking major steps towards the country's unification under the leadership of Prussia. In Russia, however, similar reforms, conducted by the Witte government failed to yield comparable results. Instead, they brought deeper crisis and social unrest culminating in the Revolution of 1905-7.

Witte's reforms were corrected by the "Stolypin Reforms" of 1906-14. Stolypin came to the conclusion that mere intervention of the state in directing market-oriented reforms was not enough. What was needed was a fundamental restructuring of the whole social fabric before List-like policies could be undertaken in the society like Russia's. Stolypin aimed at the measures that constituted a new type of "revolution from above". This stage of modernisation reforms failed as did its predecessor.

In the major upheaval that followed the failure of the "revolution from above" came what is considered a classical occurrence in the developing countries—"the revolution from below," conducted by a charismatic leader (Lenin) who rallied his followers into a party under the slogans of national independence, social emancipation, and industrial progress. The whole process of Russian transformation from Witte to Lenin can be regarded as typical to what later happened in the "developing countries." "Russia," says Shanin, "was the first country in which the syndrome of such conditions and problems appeared within the context of political independence of long standing, of successful competition in the past with the more 'modern' western neighbours, and a country possessing a numerous intellectual elite, trained in advanced European scholarship and deeply involved in social analysis and in radical political action."[76]

Regional myth

So far we have established that at the turn of the twentieth century, Russian social configuration, as we have presented it in our analysis, fitted, with certain provisions, to the existing models of the "dependent" or "developing" society. When speaking about the first of these categories, we have referred to Jowitt's remark that obsession with identity and comparisons with more modern European nations were pervasive among dependent nations, and can be seen as expressions of dependency *per se*. We would like to search for some more examples of identity-fixation and see if any other explanations can be offered.

Taking Jowitt at his word when he spoke of Romania and the whole group of peripheral countries, we shall turn to the

---

76   T. Shanin, ibidem, p. 192.

locality that may at first sight appear a stranger in this context—
the southern states of the United States of America. There is a
lot in the culture of the southern states that is remindful of the
great nineteenth century Russian culture; the very spirit of the
Southern literature—a distinct case in American literature at
large—resembles the spirit of Russian literature. Both are pre-
modern with that peculiar, perhaps a little naive, but intense
and pure *Weltschmerz*, both have that sense of phantasmagoria
of the reality, there is in both the same deep psychology and
stylistic innovation. Thus parallels can be drawn between the
created literary worlds of Faulkner and Dostoyevsky; Updike
and Styron - and Bulgakhov and Olesha.

In the literature about the American South, there is also a
persistent vision of that region as possessing its own unique
"spirit," of there being a distinct "idea" of the South.[77] The
meaning of the southern "idea" is in our view very similar to
the meaning that was attached to the Russian "idea" by Russian
religious philosophers.[78] First of all, it means an attachment to
tradition. This link of the South with tradition is expressed by
Tindall in a language that is more rational than the language
of Russian philosophers. A distinctive reality of southernism,
he says, is produced by that region's concrete historical
experience, climate, and physical setting with their impact
on its national character, the presence of the Negro culture,
the strong religious heritage, and the knowledge of good and
evil, and "the persistence of an essentially rural culture with its
neighbourliness in human relation."[79]

The opportunities before the American South, according
to Tindall, are broad, because "the land remains relatively
unspoiled, the political system is more open, and unrestrained

---

77 M. O'Brien, *The Idea of the American South*, 1920-1941, Baltimore
    1979.
78 See N. Berdiaev, *The Russian Idea*, Paris 1971.
79 B. Tindall, *The Ethnic Southerners*, Baton Rouge 1976, p. 86.

than ever before. It may be something of a cliché now, but it is also a self-evident truth, that a region so late in developing has a chance to learn from the mistakes of others."[80] Doesn't this remind us of Danilevsky's speculations about Russia? Both underscore the purity and genuineness of their respective regions and bode them a great future, not only because they are naturally predisposed to achieve one but also because they can learn from the mistakes of others that they have so far been silent observers of.

The second similarity between the Russian and the southern "idea" is an ethical component inherent in it. The American South is seen as having preserved certain key values of humanity that are steadily disappearing in the modern world.[81] Southern claims of goodness here invoke Dostoyevsky's metaphor about Russia having survived the second temptation of the Devil. Both "ideas" were at the core of what E. Garvin Davenport called "regional myths": "While the Agrarians were participating in the continuing national quest for a rehabilitation of agrarian innocence and simplicity, they professed a regional uniqueness . . . The South was the America of Jeffersonian ideals and eighteenth-century agrarianism."[82]

The third point of similarity between the two ideas is that they were both juxtaposed to their opposite parts—the South was juxtaposed to the North, and Russia was juxtaposed to Western Europe. The real meaning of this juxtaposition in the case of the South was not so much its relation to the North as its relation to the modern world. According to Current, "northernisation has

---

80 Ibidem, p. 241.
81 R.M. Weaver, *The Southern Tradition*, New Rochelle 1968.
82 F.G. Davenport, Jr., 'The Myth of Southern History: Historical Consciousness' [in:] *Twentieth-Century Southern Literature,* Nashville 1967, pp. 57-58.

generally been synonymous with modernisation."[83] As we have tried to argue throughout this work, the meaning of the Russian "idea" was very much the same.

The use of a regional myth or the regional idea of uniqueness by Russian and southern cultural elites turns in the last analysis to be a variant of culture that aims at defending virtue in the conditions of growing homogenisation, standardisation, and reduction to the lowest common denominator. Culture in these conditions is not just attached to abstract concepts, but becomes a flag that gathers around it those who are determined to defend what they see as true values.

The forming of the regional myths thus is not something specific to only one or a few nations. It appears to be a common tendency at the time of intense modernisation and the formation of nation-states. Regional myths about national uniqueness were created on the one hand as a defence mechanism against a new, strange, and standardising civilisation, and on the other hand as a mobilising symbol, allowing an entity to act in a consorted manner with an aim of occupying an appropriate position among other entities in the emerging hierarchy of the world states. To put it in Wallerstein's terms: "The extent of the debate that has gone on in the South about its 'mind', about the boundaries of the very South that is supposed to have a mind, is in fact not significantly different from comparable debates everywhere else within the time-space boundaries of the capitalist world-economy. There is nothing special about the claim to be special. There is nothing unusual about the ambiguities surrounding all the claims. The claim to specialness is part of the world-systemic political game, and it plays a central role in the operation of the system."[84]

---

83 R.N. Current, *Nothernizing the South*, Athens, Ga. 1983, pp. 12-13.

84 I. Wallerstein, 'What Can One Mean by Southern Culture' in *Geopolitics and Geoculture*, Cambridge 1991.

The English case

It transpires that Russia was not the only country in which modernity was received with a kind of shock, expressed, among other things, in the creation of a regional myth. Russia's reaction to modernity was common to many other countries in which it came from without and challenged and disrupted the traditional social patterns. The Bolshevik Revolution in Russia and the coming to power of the Nazi in Germany may be regarded as two extreme cases illustrating the reception of modernity in the regions where it was not indigenous. As we shall see, however, even the pioneer to modernisation, England, was not wholly immune to the stresses that it brought with it.

England's transition to modernity was much smoother and occurred more gradually than in other countries. Capitalist relations developed there already in an agricultural sector, and the world's first capitalist ruling class, to use a Marx's term, was British landed aristocracy and gentry. As Britain proceeded to industrialise, no straightforwardly bourgeois or industrial elite was strong enough to challenge this ruling landed aristocracy, which grew richer, more self-important and more of a consolidated oligarchy. This aristocracy however was no more feudal, but was essentially capitalist. As Perry Anderson argues, "there was thus from the start no fundamental antagonistic contradiction between the old aristocracy and the new bourgeoisie."[85]

Consequently, industrial revolution was not matched by bourgeois revolution; instead there was accommodation. However, the two classes, although being capitalist in nature, were not capitalist in the same way. The landed aristocracy who were rentiers, rather than producers or entrepreneurs, transmitted to the new middle class a certain economic passivity and aloofness. More importantly however, rentier aristocracy

---

85   P. Anderson, 'Origins of the Present Crisis,' *New Left Review*, no.23 (January-February, 1964), p. 31.

retained its cultural hegemony and was largely successful in moulding new industrial bourgeoisie after its own image.

Thus the transfer of power from landed aristocracy to the industrialists was gradual and more political than psychological. As Peregrine Worsthorne put it, it "resembled a merger rather than a conquest; a marriage (in many cases literally) rather than a rape."[86] This was a unique English development, which has no parallels in the world. If we compare it to the role played by aristocracy in, say, Germany, the differences will not be difficult to spot.

As we have pointed above, Germany began to industrialise later than England. German industrialisation proceeded with the English example in mind, and thus had an ideological element in it. It proceeded more rapidly and local bourgeoisie had less time to be absorbed into the old elite, or even to be accepted by it. There were also considerable differences between the English and the German aristocracies. The latter was reluctant to merge with wealthy businessmen and to accept them into its ranks. As a result, no accommodation took place as in the case of England and the rigour of German industrialists and entrepreneurs was not mildened by aristocratic "civilising" influences. German industrialists were not distracted from their concentration on production and German economic development was thus safeguarded in the long run.

On top of this, German aristocracy largely retained its aggressive and authoritarian military nature, which its English counterparts had already lost. Moreover, the members of the German aristocracy were not as rich as the aristocracy in England, and had to fight their way to achieve better economic and political positions. They became agrarian industrialists and often traded their political support for the governmental policies of tariff protection. Ultimately, industrial bourgeoisie

---

86 P. Worsthorne, Contribution to symposium, 'Who's Left, What's Right?' *Encounter*, March 1977, p. 29.

in Germany was not as hospitable to the ideas of liberalism and capitalism as in England, but instead favoured industrialism and greater state control.

In England where industrialisation was original and natural, its drive was nonetheless restricted by social mechanisms that evolved in response to it. English modernisation was thus self-monitored. Martin Wiener in his book, *English Culture and the Decline of English Industrial Spirit 1850-1980,* argues that immediately after the Industrial Revolution in England, public sympathies, stimulated by the views of the outspoken cultural and social elite, turned to the values of the English past, to tradition, to the simplicity of life in the countryside. This wave of anti-urbanism was not transient, but established a permanent trend in English society that served as a counterbalance to the excesses that befell many other countries on their road to modernity. The majority among the new elite, educated in the newly-emerged public schools, became averse to everything connected with technology, industrialism, and obsessive money-making. They preached the return to nature, the coming back to the ideals of rusticity, and small human community. "The new national self-image dressed itself in the trappings of an older tradition. One certain sign of the inherent self-limitations within English modernisation was the degree to which the increasingly dominant image of the nation denied its chief characteristic— the rise of industry."[87]

Wiener goes on to give numerous examples of the reaction in England against modernity expressed by industrialism, urbanisation, the spread of the values of a technocratic society, etc. This reaction is in certain respects similar to the cases already mentioned: there was a rejection of mechanistic standardising trends inherent in it. In opposition to these trends, the ideas of the return to tradition, to rural values, to the countryside were

---

87   M. Wiener, *English Culture and the Decline of the Industrial Spirit 1850-1980,* Cambridge 1981.

put forward, much in line with what happened elsewhere in the world. The difference of the English case, however, is that these counteractions came from the same source as modernisation itself. As Alan Macfarlane argues in his much discussed book,[88] modernity was very much present in the English countryside since as early as the fourteenth century: There was a market for land and labour, an early use of money in rural economy, and high levels of social and geographical mobility. The traditional pattern of the peasant society, described above and characteristic to Europe, was not, according to Macfarlane, present in England.

Since capitalism in England grew from the countryside, there was no sharp conflict between the town and the country, and by the middle of the nineteenth century, there was no longer a rural society, distinct from the "national" society based in the cities.[89] The Industrial Revolution thus may be seen as having occurred in a "uniform" society, and the trends counter to it, emanating from the same source as the main trends, served to modify and adjust, rather than violently oppose them. This is why the "regional myth" created in England was more of a narrative of a self-confident nation with an imperial past that had gone on its own way and produced its own version of a nation-state, arguably the first to be defined so, by its own means, and based on its own traditions and social dynamics. In Aristotle's terminology, the social change in England was "natural" because it had the source of movement in itself and not "by coincidence."

There is another, broader explanation of the reactions to modernisation. At the peak of it, there was a rapid growth of universalising trends, connected with the spread of rational attitudes and practices, and expressed above all in the development

---

88   See A. Macfarlane, *The Origins of English Individualism*, Oxford 1978.

89   The country-city integration is discussed in: Christopher Hill, *Reformation to Industrial Revolution: British Economy and Society, 1530-1780*, London 1967; Barrington Moore, *Social Origins of Dictatorship and Democracy*, Boston, Mass. 1966, pp. 3-39.

of science. The golden age for this was Enlightenment. It was marked by absolute preferences given to the universal against the particular, to the global against small and community-based, to reason against emotion. Around the middle of the nineteenth century, this trend was radically reversed: the particular prevailed over the universal, the national became more important than the international, and the small won over the big. This global trend, marked by the emergence of various local nationalisms and the formation of nation-states, meant that the world became more centralised into a hierarchy in which individual units vied for power, prestige, and honour.

In this emerging world structure, various individual entities were marked by their own characteristic behaviour. England, who was in the lead of modernisation, and where modernisation was an internal affair, worked out her own mechanisms to cope with the threats and challenges of it and managed to preserve the particular from the menace of the universal at the least cost. For the rest of the countries, modernisation, in the sense of institutionalisation of modernity, came from without, and each one had to cope with it in its own specific way. Everywhere, however, the latecomers to modernisation had to use the state as an instrument of social transformation, create an ideology to legitimise it, and reach out for their own cultural traditions to counterbalance its weight.

The immediate followers of English transformation, such as France, Germany, and Japan (the United States of America, as we have said, makes a special case) managed to make an appropriate use of the state, worked out a fitting ideology, and drew successfully on their cultural resources. Their transformation into dynamically evolving industrial societies thus proved to be a success. As for Russia, she found herself initially in this group of the immediate followers. She was, however, unable to activate the necessary mechanisms: neither in the structure of her state, nor in her cultural tradition could she find mechanisms that could provide a springboard for a grand leap forward. Her traditional social structure didn't allow the efficiency with which the German government utilised the misalliance between aristocracy and industrialists to promote rapid industrial growth; there was no equivalent in her culture to the ethics of samurai that played a role similar to that of the Protestant ethics in the building of modern capitalism in Japan. Having gone some way along the lines of the enlightened German reforms, she was soon forced to turn away from the outlined path. What had happened in Russia at that time bears resemblance to the events that could be observed in less developed parts of the world later in the twentieth century: there emerged a militant political movement equipped with the ideology that promised the attainment of the better of the two worlds—industrial modernisation and equality of social status. It promised to liberate vast masses of peasants and urban workers, to achieve rapid industrialisation, and raise people's standard of living. Communism, in this light, is an ideology aimed at building an institutional surrogate of modern society in the conditions of backwardness.

Grand Synthesis

Let us now try to throw some light on the factors that can account for Russia having found herself in the position of economic and social backwardness. To start with a more general one, Russia has been a part of what we now call Eastern Europe. A present-day view of Europe as being divided into the eastern and western part corresponds roughly to what became a reality after the relations of regions within the Roman Empire—the advanced East and backward West—decisively reversed. This event was noted by virtually all writers dealing with the start of the Middle Ages. The end of antiquity was marked by the Arab conquest of the two shores of the Mediterranean. The Eastern Empire became Byzantium, with a political and social system that was distinct from the rest of the European continent. It is in this setting that the change of the roles of the two parts of the Roman Empire took place. Marc Bloch wrote that "from the eighth century onwards there was a sharply demarcated group of societies in Western and Central Europe, whose elements, however diverse, were cemented solidly together by profound resemblances and constant relationship."[90] It is to this group of societies that we apply the term "feudalism" with most justification. The rest of the European continent was regarded as cultural and economic fringes. The distinction between East and West is thus registered in modern historiography as existing from the outset of the post-classical period.

What proved crucial to the destinies of the East and West was the way in which feudalism emerged in Western Europe. According to a number of western historians, the bulk of them Marxist, feudalism was a result of the grand synthesis of antiquity and pre-modern communal "mode of production" of the Germanic tribes. Both of them were undergoing the process of decay, but their fusion transmitted a new dynamic to the development of Western Europe. The role of Graeco-Roman civilisation in this synthesis was mainly cultural. Due to the use of slave labour, the elites of the antiquity had leisure to occupy themselves with the matters of high culture and politics. In ancient Greece, the absolute notion of "liberty" was singled out from the political continuum of relative conditions and rights that had existed before it. Likewise, Roman civilisation, by elaborating the norms of civil law, separated the pure notion of "property" from the spectrum of indeterminate "possession" that had preceded it.

The German tribes contributed to this fusion the pattern of their social organisation. The communal enclaves of the medieval village are believed to be a Germanic inheritance,

---

90   M. Bloch. *Melanges Historiques,* Paris 1963, vol.1, p. 123.

the leftovers of the original rural systems of the forest. At the peak of the medieval polity, the institution of the feudal monarchy was itself initially an amalgam of the Germanic war-leader, who was semi-elective and possessed rudimentary secular functions, and the Roman imperial ruler, who was a sacred autocrat with unlimited powers and responsibilities.

The important function in this synthesis was that of the Christian Church. It provided for the continuity in the conditions in which different structures and institutions merged and changed their character. It served as the main channel through which the cultural values of the classical world flowed into the new realities of feudal Europe, where literacy had become clerical. The Christian Church may be said to have launched the universalising trends long before they became amplified by the emergence of the mechanisms specific to modernity. It ruptured the elusive union between man and nature that marked the art and philosophy of the classical antiquity; the western monastic orders transmitted to human labour the divine dignity, from which it was devoid in the antiquity when work was associated purely with slaves; with the christianisation of the Roman Empire, the speech of the mass of the rural population was latinised, producing the Romance languages, which became one of the essential social bonds of continuity between antiquity and the Middle Ages.

If we now turn to Eastern Europe, it followed a different pattern of development. According to Perry Anderson: "the most fundamental characteristic of the whole planar zone stretching from the Elbe to the Don can be defined as the permanent *absence* of that specific western synthesis between a disintegrating tribal-communal mode of production based on primitive agriculture and dominated by rudimentary warrior aristocracies, and a dissolving slave mode of production, with an extensive urban civilisation based on commodity exchange, and an imperial State system. This central fact was the basic historical determinant of the uneven development of Europe, and of the persistent retardation of the East."[91]

Another feature that slowed down the development of Eastern Europe was the pressure of nomadic pastoralism. The vicinity of the steppes and fierce attacks from the nomadic tribes significantly retarded the internal evolution of the agrarian societies of this region. For a long time, tribe and clan were the basic units of social organisation; paganism remained untouched; methods of soil cultivation were primitive. Gradually, however, the social structure became more complex and political stratification began to take place. As agrarian techniques began to improve, the access to and the manner of disposal of the produced surplus stimulated the emergence of a warrior nobility, which started to exercise power over small peasantry. Princes and chiefs with their armed retinues soon became a stable ruling class. In the wake of this maturation of the social and political structure, there began to emerge in the ninth and tenth centuries numerous small towns that combined the function of trade with that of defence. When Scandinavians came to Russia, they were impressed by the number of trade towns there. The emergence of towns in Eastern Europe may thus be considered as the highest endogenous achievement of this region during the Dark Ages.

Further development of Eastern Europe cannot be understood properly without a link to its western part. As Perry Anderson wrote: "The continental proximity of more advanced economic and social systems adjacent to it must always be remembered in assessing the course of events in Eastern Europe itself. The profound influence these exercised, in different ways, on the political structures and state systems of the medieval East, can be seen from the consistency of the philological evidence for it. Thus virtually all key Slavonic words for higher political rank and domination in this period—the vocabulary of the state

---

91   P. Anderson, *Passages From Antiquity to Feudalism,* London 1974, p. 213.

superstructure itself—are derived from Germanic, Latin or Turanian terms."[92]

When speaking about specific features of the East, it must be remembered that there were significant variations within this region. The specificity of Russia lay in her greater proximity to Asia and thus in greater exposure to the influences of nomadism. The shock that she experienced during the prolonged rule of savage Mongol tribes left a deep wound in the national psyche and did not pass without its effect on the social structure and methods of state administration. What adds up to Russia's complexity is that something of the western synthesis does seem to have occurred there. The main cultural impetus for the first Russian state came from Byzantium. It is from Byzantium that the two main components for an ideological system were borrowed—written language and religion. Together with the adoption of the Orthodox faith, the Byzantine institution of a state church was also adopted, which was later to become the medium of ideological transplantation of the autocratic imperial tradition of the Eastern Empire, even after the latter ceased to exist. The administrative and cultural influence of Byzantium thus allows the proposition that there was a Russian version of the western synthesis. We should bear in mind, however, that there was no common geographical territory between Kiev and Byzantium that could enable an actual fusion.

Given the overwhelming numerical predominance of peasants over other social strata at the start of Russia's transformation to modernity, there was no social agent capable of transforming Russian Orthodoxy into an ethical religion,[93] as was the case with the western branch of Christianity. According to Weber, peasants are usually so strongly tied to nature and

---

92 P. Anderson, ibidem, p.231.
93 By "ethical religion" we mean what Max Weber called *Alltagsreligiositaet*, i.e. the introduction of moral religious norms into the routine of everyday life.

so dependent on organic processes, that they become carriers of religion only in extreme circumstances, i.e., when they are threatened by enslavement or proletarianisation. As a general rule, peasantry remained involved with weather-magic and animistic-magic or ritualism; insofar as it worked out an ethical religion, the focus was on a purely formalistic ethic in relation to god and priests.

Our stereotype of the peasant as being a god-fearing and pious man is a thoroughly modern phenomenon. The religious glorification of the peasant and the belief in the special worth of his piety were characteristic of Russian nineteenth century religiosity tied with Slavophile influences. It appeared as the reaction against capitalism and modern socialism. These Russian populists, or *narodniki*, also tried to link the anti-rationalist protest of intellectuals with the revolt of the countryside against the bureaucratic church, surrounding both intellectual and agrarian protest with a religious aura. The emphasis on peasant religiosity thus served ideological needs of Russian intelligentsia. The emergence of real religious ethic was not possible in the countryside. As Max Weber wrote, "The specific qualities of Christianity as an ethical religion of salvation and as personal piety found their real nurture in the urban environment; and it is there that they created new movements time and again, in contrast to the ritualistic, magical or formalistic re-interpretation favoured by the dominant feudal powers."[94]

The natural carriers of religious ethic according to Weber are the members of the middle class, such as merchants, artisans, etc., who systematically rely in their dealings on honesty and contractual reciprocity. The relative lack of such class in Russia may account for the inability of Russian Christianity to spread as an ethical religion, regulating the events of an everyday life. It is perhaps because of this

---

94   M. Weber, *Economy and Society*, New York 1968, vol. 3, p. 472.

deficiency, that such a prominent role in Russian social life was played by a quasi-proletarian or "proletaroid" as Weber calls it, intelligentsia. They undertook to fill the vacuum and worked out the doctrines that combined rational knowledge with quasi-religious fervour, which can be seen as a substitute of a religious ethic.

Good people—Evil Empire

The fact about Russia that is broadly agreed upon is an undeniable goodness of the people living there and the over-bureaucratised, insensitive, and often aggressive and expansionist nature of her state. The modernisation theory as we have proposed to treat it in this work clarifies in our opinion some of the reasons for such view.

Modernisation as it spread from the regions where it originated, i.e., from the countries of Western Europe, was nowhere received in a calm and neutral manner. As we have seen, all countries reacted to its assertive and decisive appearance with a kind of shock—the greater in the farther-off corners of the world, and the lesser in its centres. The countries of the world's periphery characteristically responded to it by creating regional myths that expressed their horror at the possibility of losing the values to which they had grown accustomed over the course of centuries. The myths that were created were intended to "re-enchant" the world that became "disenchanted," to hide away from the cold winds that brought new and unfamiliar values, norms, and relations. The lower the societies stood on the ladder of the world hierarchy, i.e. the closer they were to simple and nature-bound forms of social life, the stranger new trends seemed to them and the more painful was the response of these societies to the encroaching modernity.

Max Weber, describing the meaning of the war dance to the primitive communities, wrote that it was initially performed with a mixture of fury and fear that produced heroic frenzy.[95] Later on, the war dance developed into a ritual for building up military spirit and strengthening morale. The first encounter of the peripheral societies with modernity may be compared with the behaviour of the primitive peoples in a war dance. When modern attitudes and practices began to spread in these societies, the reaction to them was deep mistrust combined with fear and an instinctual drive to defend themselves. A real-life example of such reaction is always at hand: a young girl working in a shop in Moscow or Vologda may be rude and unpleasant to the customers, not because she is wicked or ill-brought up, but because she has not come to terms with her role of a formal and anonymous agent in a modern commercial enterprise. Her rudeness or even aggressiveness (much spoken of as being a characteristic feature of the Russian service) may be but a "war dance" in the face of the conceived dangers awaiting her in pursuance of her formal functions. To be sure, she may be the most sweet and charming person at home, among her close friends and relatives, and in situations where no impersonal roles are involved.

The same can refer to other situations requiring formal and impersonal behaviour: the work of state bureaucrats, public officials, clerks of all sorts, etc. What produces such attitudes is the traditional mentality of a small peasant community that draws a sharp line between those who are inside and those who are outside, the friends and the enemies, *us* and *them*. Those inside the community are friends, those outside are not just strangers—they are potential enemies. The facial gloominess of Muscovites, so striking to the western visitors to this town may be compared with "hate stare," which, as Goffman notes,[96] whites in the southern United States were known to give to blacks in public places as a sign of their rejection of

---

95   See M. Weber, *Sociology of Religion*, London 1965.
96   Erving Goffman, *Behavior in Public Places*, New York 1963.

the right of blacks to participate in the day-to-day interaction with whites. The "routine benevolence," characteristic to the members of modern society, where the variety of encounters occur in the anonymous settings and require a measure of polite estrangement, or what Goffman has called "civil inattention," is lacking in the societies that still preserve traditional attitudes and postures. These attitudes strictly suggest the vision of a human being as a "whole person," not divisible into social roles. This "wholeness" is considered a highest virtue and as an indication of moral integrity and genuineness of character, while western "civil inattention" is taken for coldness of temper, moral indifference, calculated rationality, and even wickedness. With this insight in mind, the accusations laid by Dostoyevsky and other Slavophiles on the West appear in a new light and the moral fervour of Russian past and present nationalists becomes more understandable.

The persistence in Russia of peasant-based attitudes can also account for her policies that have earned her the reputation of "Evil Empire." As we have seen from the above, "good people" can suddenly become aggressive when they decide that they are dealing with outsiders. Their reaction is perfectly natural to them since they expect the worst from the strangers. Ever since the modern world system started to establish itself, Russia was doomed to perform the "war dance." Her actions on the international arena were often dictated by her perceived necessity to adhere to the virtues of honour and martial heroism. When she was successful at playing a role of a great power, she was accepted as such by the members of the international community. The falling apart of the Soviet Union and a subsequent political and economic chaos injured Russia's reputation in the eyes of the world. All of a sudden she was forced to switch from the role of a mighty, well-organised, self-confident empire to a country enfeebled by numerous social and economic maladies, while trying to formulate her new role in the world politics.

It was then that hitherto hidden characteristics of Russia as a dependent and developing society came to broad daylight. All of a sudden, the people of former Soviet republics faced the moment of truth and began to see the real mechanisms of social action and human motivation. The highly-placed preachers of order, elevated social ideals, and strict morality turned into plain folk, struggling for their place in life. There appeared new leaders—heralds of radical liberalism, defensive supporters of former ideals, cynical and defiant businessmen, or ardent nationalists. The orderly streets of towns and cities filled with petty traders selling their humble merchandise in defiance of previous norms that held individual entrepreneurship in utter contempt of morality as well as law. The television programs turned into orgies of hitherto prohibited mass arts and battlegrounds for politicians of all sorts using all sorts of dirty tricks; there appeared a new brand of people, driving in fancy cars and dining in expensive restaurants; there also appeared new losers, begging in the streets, queuing for jobs, and watching the newly rich with the desperation of envy. Crime came fully into the public view and the word "Mafia" ceased to apply just to some distant reality or Hollywood.

Ever since the Gorbachev-led breakthrough, the process of routinisation of democracy has proceeded in a wave-like fashion. The initial euphoria about the newly-acquired freedom was replaced with the feeling of doubt and uncertainty as to where to go next. The bald slogans of economic and political liberals suddenly began to sound suspicious and unrealistic. The western-oriented extravaganza in mass media gradually gave way to restrained, nostalgic, inward-looking, self-searching, meditative attitude. After several years of orgiastic displays of western mass entertainment, the New Year's Eve television broadcasts, which up until then brought the nation together in absence of stable, historically-bred traditions and ceremonials, turned in the last couple of years into the replicas of quiet and warm-hearted gatherings of good friends, which through the sixties and seventies were called "Novogodnij Ogoniok," or "New Year Candle Light." The "Ogonioks" of 1996 and 1997 were a complete turn away from their predecessors in the Gorbachev-initiated era. The biggest Russian pop stars suddenly abandoned their aspirations to look and sound like their counterparts in the west and came out with the looks and repertoire of the Soviet artists of the sixties. It seems that by reproducing that idyllic atmosphere, permeated with warmth, *naiveté*, and human touch, so distant from the rationality, formality, and social Darwinism of the encroaching capitalism, Russian intelligentsia made another attempt to "go back to the roots," rediscover the national self, and "re-enchant" the world that had grown cold.

Similar twists also could be observed in Russian politics. The ardent liberals like Gaidar were replaced with disoriented conservatives like Chernomyrdin, only to be reinforced with yet another generation of liberals like Nemtsov. Such oscillations are likely to continue for some time until finally the Russian political scene becomes stabilised, with two or three major political groupings with distinct outlooks being formed in place of the present multicolour variety of parties and eccentric political personalities. It is probably then, that the world will see the new Russia—stable, self-assured, at one with, yet different from the west. The alternative to that is also plain—the country in "permanent transition," the transition that never ends.

Conclusion

To sum up the main points of this work, in the late nineteenth century, Russia found herself in the situation in which she had to give her reaction to new trends coming from the western countries and formulate her stance in relation to other entities making up the contemporaneous world. These new trends made up the intensified version of what later was conceptualised as "modernity." Politically, the world was turning into a hierarchy of states in which economically advanced and politically well-organised countries were dictating the rest of the world on which path to proceed. They did that by the example of their achievements in technology and culture, but also by the threat and use of force that itself had grown in power and concentration. The mid-nineteenth century was a turning point in the sense that the main trends of modernity that had been accumulating for several centuries burst out in torrents of breakthroughs. The institutionalisation of modernity involved, among its main dimensions, the creation of a modern nation-state with an unprecedented administrative concentration, the control of information and social supervision, and also with a distinctive cultural outlook caused by the merger of two entities that had hitherto remained separate—territorial and ethnic.[97]

The process of formation of a nation-state went along with other institutional dimensions of modernity—industrialisation, growth of capitalism, development of science, increase in military power caused by "industrialisation of war," etc. The effect of

---

97 See E. Gellner, *Nations and Nationalism*, Oxford 1983.

these modern institutions on human consciousness was almost universally one of great shock and the reaction of defence. The modes of defence differed with each separate culture and each socio-political model. The emerging nation-states of Western Europe that started to modernise first dealt with the dangers and excesses of modernisation by counterbalancing it with cultural and religious responses directed towards containing it within a controllable framework. Modernisation, being more of their internal affair, proceeded there in a self-monitored fashion. Thus in England, the Industrial Revolution with the standardising and levelling effects that it produced, was followed by a massive return of the population to the values of the countryside, to tradition, to the simple ideals of rusticity, and the small, human community. Socially, there occurred an accommodation rather than a conflict between new industrialists and old country nobility, allowing for the building in England of an industrial society with a "human face."

Elsewhere in the world, things did not go so smoothly. The responses of the latecomers to modernity may be grouped into three main models[98] (once again we exclude the United States as a special case): Prusso-Japanese, Russian, and Islamic. In Germany and Japan, social elites have successfully conducted modern reforms by mobilising their societies along the lines of transformation ideology, using the mechanisms of the strong state, and drawing on the resources of their respective cultural and religious traditions. It should be noted, that the role of the state in these countries was historically very strong. Some explanation of why it was so in Germany was given above. As for Japan, the Confucian tradition undoubtedly played its role. Furthermore, both countries had worked out an ethical religion in the sense of what Max Weber called *Alltagsreligiosität*, i.e., religious norms for use in everyday life.

---

98 This classification is taken from Ernest Gellner's lectures delivered in Warsaw in 1994.

The Russian response was also on the elite level. However, it did not follow the Prusso-Japanese model. Instead, its essence was the split of the Russian elite into two opposite militant ideological camps—pro-western liberals (Westerners) and nationalist conservative populists (Slavophiles). Being thus radically polarised, the Russian elite failed to spell out a coherent ideology of modern transformation and after a series of attempts at conducting German-like reforms, they left the field to the new corporate social actor—the Bolsheviks.

The third reaction to modernity did not concern us in this work. It is of interest, however, as the reaction on the part of one of the world's three greatest religions—Islam. The reaction of Islam to the modernising world was the cutting off from it and reaching for inner reserves of Islamic religion that resulted in its extreme radicalisation. There have always simultaneously existed two brands of Islam: High Islam—prophetic, puritanical, and scripturalist, and Low Islam—ritualistic, orgiastic, and mediated by priests.[99] The reaction to modernity was the advancement of the former at the expense of the latter. Different as social and institutional processes were in the core and the periphery, the reaction to modernity by two great world religions appear uniform—Islam, as well as Christianity, went through a Reformation, each in its own way and at different points in time.

Russia, as we have pointed out, was unable to utilise the mechanisms that proved efficient for the modern transformation of Germany and Japan. Her fragmented elite did not offer a coherent modernisation ideology, the state did not modernise to the extent that it could exercise effective administrative control necessary for large-scale comprehensive reforms, there turned out to be little in Russian national tradition that could be activated as a driving force of change, and Russian Orthodoxy failed to emerge as an ethical religion guiding the everyday conduct. In the face of the lack of these mechanisms, they had to

---

99   See E. Gellner, *Muslim Society*, Cambridge 1981.

be substituted. The communist rule was one great, institutional surrogate of modernity. Being unable to modernise with the help of the above mechanisms and being under the increasing pressure from the outside world to modernise anyway, Russia made an attempt to exercise a great leap into modernity by using social engineering on a hitherto unseen scale. It was an attempt at denying the laws of social gravitation and rejecting social physics as such. We can call the communist experiment a "Baron Münhausen act," which brings to mind a personage of German fairy tales who boasted to be able to lift himself by grabbing hold of his own hair.

Communism as an institutional surrogate of modernity was not the first or the only surrogate that was produced in the course of Russian history. It was the aim of this work to show a number of such surrogates in Russian social life, economy, literature, and culture at large. It is our thesis that the creation of such surrogates, the mixing of modern and traditional elements, is a phenomenon common to the countries trying to catch up with those holding the positions of leadership in technological and social development. According to Immanuel Wallerstein, since the early sixteenth century, the world has been moving in one particular direction set by the dynamics of global economy that has been essentially capitalist. The performance in global economy has created a hierarchy of world states and has forced the imposition of core-like institutional formats on the periphery. Along with this, there has been another powerful factor responsible for the diffusion of modern values and attitudes. It is what could be called "Protestant world culture." The spread of it by modern mass media and the under-surface influence it exercised on the communist regimes is one of the chief factors accounting for their spectacular downfall.

In the situation when the prospect of marginalisation and "thirdworldism" began to loom large on the horizon, Russia began to struggle hard to recover her erstwhile reputation of a great power. New political elites took to the policies of pragmatism and political bargaining. Again, these new measures are more visible on the international arena than at home. With Russia's present weakened position, however, things do not proceed as smoothly as she may wish them to. NATO *has* gone ahead with bringing in new members no matter what Russia has said to it. Russia's objections to intervention in Serbia and her principled stand towards other policies directed by the United States, together with major European states, have been repeatedly disregarded. She has found herself increasingly isolated in sticking to her peculiar principles based, as Russian diplomats have persistently claimed, on the standards and norms of international law. In their recourse to the United Nations Charter, Russian diplomats have been drawing upon the word and letter of law more than on its essence and spirit. Russia's failure to come to terms with and understand the position of the United States and Great Britain in the United Nations Security Council is basically caused by the belief in immutability and transcendent nature of law as expressed in a legal system or a code. Russian political regime, in times of the tsar's as well as communist rulers, has used law as the legitimation of a regime and not as mechanism regulating the relations between citizens. As such, law was viewed as a sacrosanct expression of some absolute spirit of justice, not to be interpreted or amended by human beings.

Such perception of law, rooted in European thought and practice and common to most of the continental European states, is inherently at odds with the Anglo-Saxon perception expressed in the system of common law and grounded in the belief that what is at stake is a notion of justice that is reproduced by interpreting basic assumptions about living together that is adopted by the majority of citizens in a codified or non-codified form. Now that law has come to regulate the relations of nations formerly thought to exist in the Hobbesian "state of nature," there occurs a clash of attitudes towards law, which is expressive of deep-rooted cultural and social traditions. Russia's position in the Security Council often depicts a tendency to stick to an article of law and not see a real problem that this article is called to regulate. In such an approach, law as a system of rules is separated from the reality on the ground and takes precedence before considerations of justice.

One does not have to be a Freudian to view with suspicion such a proclaimed attachment to law. Especially by representatives of a state in which the disregard of legal matters and the manipulation of laws has had a long history. This is why President Putin's call on his second election to office in 2004 to establish a "dictatorship of law" caused some outcry and accusations of dictatorial propensities. Once again, as during the period that Danilevsky mentions in his book, Russia perceives herself to be misunderstood, her right actions are felt to be disregarded, and opposed by morally and legally dubious actors.

Two decades into the post-communist transition, Russia has certainly changed, however slowly the process has been taking place. Her political life has become more vibrant and inclusive. The political parties led by Zhirinovsky and Zyuganov have managed to gain enough elbow room to make the ruling party, *United Russia,* worry about how the next election results would turn out. The elections themselves have turned into grand spectacles like in the West and ever more people seem to care about who will hold the reigns of power. The grass root actions on the streets of Moscow and the reactions to them on the part of the government so far have not turned too ugly and this is a testimony to the way a civil society is emerging in Russia. The leaders of this new civil society are the cultural elites of Russia, the same category of people who in the past had stimulated the rest of the nation and showed them the way ahead. The debates held on television are very often first class in terms of quality of arguments and allusions to history and social sciences. Bad-tempered as these debates often turn out to be, they still show the characteristically Russian passion for truth and the solution of the nagging problems. They also show that the great Russian culture still prompts the way, digests the perceptions of reality, and prepares the ground for the *citizen* to become the defining characteristic of the human being living in that country. In this, the culture can only help. Weren't the American founding fathers deeply cultured men? Was it not a tradition in Central and Eastern Europe for men of culture to lead the political movements? In this sense, Vaclav Havel is more representative than Lech Walesa and more accordant with Eastern European political trends.

On the other hand, Russia has found herself in the category of states with which she was not associated before. The other so-called BRIC countries—Brazil, India, and China—not only lie thousands of miles away from Russia, but belong to different civilisations. Russia, although thought by some as being a Euro-Asiatic nation, in virtue of being placed both in Europe and in Asia, and having certain traits of social structure characteristic of Asian nations, culturally and politically has always been closely connected to Europe. As a great power, she used to play a pivotal role in European politics and her culture has, not only drawn on and sustained itself by the culture of Europe, but made a great contribution to the latter and has always been considered as an integral part of it. The nostalgia and spiritual longing of the famous Russian intellectuals, or intelligentsia as they came to be called, has always been directed towards Europe—continental Europe first of all, the British cultural influence being weak or undefined.

After centuries of struggling to occupy her due place in the world hierarchy and various ups and downs on this way, Russia seems to have reached the point where her real worth has been put to the test. She hasn't been ranked as a first-class European nation on a par with France or Germany, she has lost her weight and authority among lesser European nations, even among former constituents of the Soviet Empire, and has been lumped together with countries widely thought to be of a third world and developing category. Even in this group, her position is dubious. Whereas the other three have made their breakthrough by resorting to their inner human and social resources and technological innovation, Russia has relied mainly on her natural riches and the prices they receive on global markets. Neither the Chinese model of export-led growth and cheap labour, nor the Indian way of diligent, disciplined, intelligent, bilingual, and reasonably priced workforce, nor the Brazilian way of spirited social experimentation conjoined with openness to innovation and supported by vast natural resources, have found any substantial ground in Russia.

The ideals the Russian intellectuals have aspired to have been first and foremost the continental European "aristocratic" ideals of human destiny and social organisation. Those are the ideals many of the leading continental European thinkers themselves have struggled to revise. In doing this, they even placed hopes and relied on Russian intellectuals to be unburdened by European intellectual backlog and capable of thinking and doing things in a new way. Russia, however, remained too much of a good pupil to become an authoritative teacher. The critique and even contempt of outdated and hackneyed European ways that Russian intellectuals could share with Anglo-Saxon thinkers did not lead to new approaches and solutions. Having been at certain points in time on the cutting edge of space technology, basic and applied sciences, arts, music, and literature, and some would say experiments in social administration, Russia seems to have settled to pursue a role of a quiet, authoritative, middle-class nation more intent on taking care of its own citizens than playing the active role of a world's giant. Being a giant is not such a thrilling and prestigious thing any more. Some of the present-day giants do not appear very attractive whereas certain dwarfs seem to have it all. And what is the point to look and be different when even the French say that we are all Americans now?

Toned down as Russian aspirations for greatness seem to be in today's globalised world, her great culture and sensibilities of her people to essential issues of human existence still hold a potential for her to play an important role on the world stage. The more Russia connects with the rest of the world, the more she interacts with others in different spheres of social life and politics, the more she becomes aware of her place among others, the more she is ready to develop and move forward.

Selected Bibliography

Anderson, Perry, *Passages From Antiquity to Feudalism*, London 1974.

Bakhtin, M.M., *Problemy poetiki Dostoyevskogo*, Moscow 1963.

Berger, Peter, *The Capitalist Revolution*, New York 1986.

Chaadaev, Piotr, *Izbrannye sotchinienia i pis'ma*, Moscow 1991.

Danilevsky, N.Y., *Rossia i Evropa*, Moscow 1869.

Gellner, Ernest, *Nations and Nationalism*, Oxford 1983.

Giddens, Anthony, *The Consequences of Modernity*, Stanford 1990.

Jowitt, Kenneth, *The Leninist Response to National Dependency*, Berkeley 1976.

Kliucevsky, V.O., *Kurs russkoi istorii*, Moscow 1987.

Macfarlane, Alan, *The Origins of English Individualism*, Oxford 1978.

Mann, Michael, *The Rise and Decline of the Nation State,* Cambridge 1990.

Shanin, Teodor, *Peasants and Peasant Societies,* Oxford 1971.

Shanin, Teodor, *Russia as a Developing Society*, Oxford 1985.

Walicki, Andrzej, *Aleksander Herzen. Kwestia polska i geneza pewnych stereotypow* , Warsaw 1991.

Wallerstein, Immanuel, *The Politics of the World-Economy*, Cambridge 1984.

Wallerstein, Immanuel, *Geopolitics and Geoculture*, Cambridge 1991.

Weber, Max, *Economy and Society*, New York 1968.

Weber, Max, *The Sociology of Religion*, London 1965.

Wiener, Martin, *English Culture and the Decline of the Industrial Spirit 1850-1980*, Cambridge 1981.

www.ingramcontent.com/pod-product-compliance
Lightning Source LLC
Chambersburg PA
CBHW020539290526
45786CB00002B/961